OUT FLEW THE
Butterfly

BY
ALISON RYAN-CHASE

Conscious Dreams
PUBLISHING

Out Flew The Butterfly

Copyright © 2025: Alison Ryan-Chase

All rights reserved. No part of this publication may be produced, distributed, or transmitted in any form or by any means, including photocopying, recording, or other electronic or mechanical methods, without the prior written permission of the publisher, except in the case of brief quotations embodied in critical reviews and certain other non-commercial uses permitted by copyright law.

I have tried to recreate events, locales and conversations from my memories of them. In order to maintain their anonymity in some instances I have changed the names of individuals and places, I may have changed some identifying characteristics and details such as physical properties, occupations and places of residence.

Published by Conscious Dreams Publishing
www.consciousdreamspublishing.com

Edited by Elise Abram and Daniella Blechner
Typeset and E-book formatting by Amit Dey

ISBN: 978-1-917584-59-3

DEDICATION

I thank the Holy Trinity, first and foremost.
No matter what, God already knew the outcome.

I also dedicate this book to my wonderful parents, Malcolm and Esther Ryan, and to my siblings, who have loved me unconditionally and always had my back.

To my children, who showed me the epiphany of love —
I am ever so blessed to be called their mother.
And to their father, who has believed in me and loved me throughout the journey of life.

CONTENTS

Introduction vii

PART 1: Introducing Dookie Dooks 1
Chapter 1: Weeding the Soil... Apology Selfie! 3
Chapter 2: Ears That Heard and Eyes That Saw 15

PART 2: Teenage Years 27
Intro 29
Chapter 3: It's Only a Game 31
Chapter 4: The Highs & Lows of High School 49
Chapter 5: Kilburn Poly's Blackjack Punishment! 59
Chapter 6: Is This Love That I'm Feelin'? 69

PART 3: To Have And To Hold 81
Chapter 7: Who's That Guy? 83
Chapter 8: Weak In One Week 93

Chapter 9: Broth vs Mangoes! 109

Chapter 10: Clear Blue. 123

Chapter 11: First 135

Chapter 12: To Have and To Hold 147

Chapter 13: It's All About the Temperature 163

Chapter 14: When Passions Overflow 177

Chapter 15: Nine and a Half Weeks 191

Chapter 16: Home Sweet Home 203

Chapter 17: How Do You Say Goodbye? 219

Chapter 18: A Walk to Revelation 229

Chapter 19: What Did You Do Maria? 247

Chapter 20: Gifts of a Revival 265

About the Author 291

INTRODUCTION

As adults, we yearn to go back to our childhoods, when life was less complicated. There was an element of freedom, free to play, free to explore, and no bills or debts to worry about. The only relationship problems we had were fallings out with friends over toys. It's also fair to say that not everybody's childhood was blissful. Abuse comes in many forms, emotional, physical, sexual and spiritual and it isn't until adulthood that we reap the harvest of such.

For years I scribbled down my hurt and pain, my joy and laughter, my hopes and dreams, my failures, and yes, my successes, down in notepads, books, diaries, old schoolbooks—anywhere I could. Why? Because I always felt I needed to archive my memories, frightened I'd forget. Although some things needed to be forgotten, I knew that one day I'd want to somehow put it all together and turn it into a valuable book or something.

My love for creative writing as a young girl always had me writing stories or little poems, sometimes from actual events, and I would add a little twist or just allow my imagination to run wild. All of this led to a compulsion to share, not just to release but to encourage many others whom I believe are going through all kinds of 'stuff'.

Realising I'd been sold a dream by the fairy tale stories and Walt Disney movies as a child, slowly, as I experienced life, I experienced reality. I came to a realisation one day that there had to be a reason why my life derailed from the fairy tale I imagined as a child: my choices in relationships, my fears, my hang-ups. I looked back and discovered roots in my childhood, a liberating time of self-reflection understanding and accepting the woman I'd become. Unlocking the closet and tackling the ghosts one by one made me the woman I became. My path into adulthood was one that had me understanding my personality and not being so hard on myself.

Be it two years to old age, whatever it was that happened in our youth can keep us in bondage for the rest of our lives. No matter when the seeds were planted, they create a cycle of behaviour, and unless we go back and deal with them, rooting them up, they will mess with and direct the decisions and destinies of our futures. We need to go back to break off the stems of all the false lies, bearing in mind that in adulthood, we can't always fix what was broken in our childhoods. We want the intimate relationships we lacked in our youth, to be close to someone as adults because we never had that closeness as children.

I went back to a place of vulnerability to dissolve all the messages that told me I was nothing, that nobody wanted me, and I was ugly. Messages that told me to believe the lie that to be indecently touched equalled love and all of the other lies that influenced me while growing up.

My injured soul advised me in negative ways, ways that made me abuse myself. I needed a renewal of my mind. There were thoughts that my siblings didn't love me (lies), that receiving love meant giving myself freely to please abusive men, opening the door to sexual encounters (lies). I was drawn to people who put me down and who were highly critical, but I had to take it because that was what I was used to (lies). It was not normal, it was not right, and none of it was my fault.

Relationships are meant to complement, not complete! The man should bring his best, and the woman should bring her best, and together, they should complement each other. I learnt this the hard way, as you'll see, by not being able to speak up for myself and my desires and needs, my fear of asking for something due to a fear of rejection, never getting the reinforcement that I was worthy and an increased lack of self-confidence.

As a child, there was the sense that some actions and situations were not okay, yet that voice—always that voice—said it was fine to go with the flow, to stay quiet, to do as I was told.

So many false truths and lies manifested over the years. I was chasing love by chasing the wrong types of guys.

The Greek word for truth is 'reality.' My childhood had a falseness to it. This came from the 'lies' Later in life, I would come to understand that satan is the father of lies and Jesus is the Way, the Truth and the Light.

My parents loved me; my siblings loved me—that was truth; that was reality. Reality came and put the truth in me, and the lies slowly eroded away... but was it too late?

Through ramblings and poetry, my words express that which I suppressed, my soul crying out in an apology to myself for the direction my life took as a young woman.

You, the reader, will be encouraged, knowing that you are not alone. Could it be that I was not the only little girl who believed my future would be happy-go-lucky with a prince by my side for a happily-ever-after? Have you ever repeatedly made bad choices in relationships? Do you have hang-ups? Are you always fearful? Don't be scared. Search for your healing and learn to accept who you are.

My drama is not over, but I am an overcomer, and I am still overcoming it!

This book takes you back to my childhood with little pockets of memories, back to happy times when I felt loved.

My cousin gave me the little pet name 'Dookie Dooks'. Heaven knows why or what it meant, but when it was used, it made me feel so special and safe. Then, there were memories that opened the doors I kept tightly locked. Present and past pain over my teenage and adult years really did have a foundation; it had a root: the seeds sown in the soil of my childhood. Not all seeds bloom into flowers; some grow into weeds or roses with thorns.

Let's go gardening. Bring your gloves—it's going to get dirty!

Part 1

Introducing Dookie Dooks

Chapter 1

WEEDING THE SOIL... APOLOGY SELFIE!

Dear Dookie Dooks,

Yes, that was one of your childhood nicknames I remember you had, given to you by your favourite cousin in America. Having a nickname made you feel loved and accepted. It made you smile every time you heard it with that American accent. I know you looked up to that cousin as she had so much mouth; she knew how to stick up for herself.

The trouble is, when you tried to be sassy and answer back to your older brothers and sister, you were seen as the little brat sister; I guess a female version of Joseph without the dreams! Your parents always stuck up for you. Being the youngest, your older siblings always got into trouble as soon as you cried. I know you didn't think it harmful as you were only 5–6 years old, but you became an annoying sister instead of an accepted in the clan, and it was that time when you were visiting with your mum's brother, Uncle Ellon, that you realised your siblings feelings towards you.

All of your siblings and cousins were in the back room, sitting and chatting as they did, and you were playing hide-and-seek with your cousin, who was similar to your age. You snuck into the room and hid behind a sofa, and then you heard them: 'Harry is so cute. You're so lucky to have him as a baby brother. Maria is such a brat—can't stand her—and so ugly she makes me sick,' and you froze. You couldn't move, you couldn't open your mouth, you just kneeled in your position and stayed hidden whilst they spoke horrible things about you. You wanted to cry, but to cry meant that you'd heard, and you decided to pretend that you hadn't heard a word. I sealed your mouth, and as Harry ran into the room looking for you, I made you jump out of your hiding place with your first-ever mask, smiling and giggling with Harry and joyfully saying, 'You're it,' running out of the room with your ears hearing the whispers: 'Do you think she heard? Was she there all the time?' I shut you up and showed you how to pretend not to hear. I sealed your mouth and shut your eyes so the tears welling up under the lids would not be seen as proof that you'd heard every word.

The little girl all of the aunts and uncles thought was adorable and had so much grown-up chit-chat beyond her years was a nobody to her siblings and cousins, always wanting to fit in and people please, to be liked and loved.

I'm sorry. Sorry that I made you feel like hiding away and sorry that I made you kneel in your hiding spot and listen to all that talk. I should have made you jump up or make a sound so they'd know you were there. They might have stopped talking before you heard those damaging words. I'm sorry that whilst your insides were broken-hearted and you cried internally, I made you pretend and suppress your feelings, and they just rooted and grew with you. I'm sorry I didn't protect you, Dookie Dooks, but you were and still are loved very much.

Now that you are a woman, know that this is where it began. Please forgive me.

Yours sincerely,

Me!

I LEARNT TO SHUT UP!

What's the point having a voice? Shut up!
Every opinion you have to express brings a shouting match —
you have no defence... Shut up!
Blood ties make no sense; they sit on the opposition's fence,
making life more tense... Shut up!
You wanna speak up? Shut up!
You wanna talk about what? Shut up!
SHUT UP.

Well, it's time to remove the seal
And backwards start to peel off the bandage of bondage
Take the mask off, and keep it real
Speak out in a love language
Of forgiveness and self-discovery
In search of the me that, as a caterpillar
Crept into a cocoon
Tired of being on such a low level
Aspiring to aim higher
The devil is a liar
Metamorphosis is taking place
And when it's over
Wings shall fly out in grace.
Talk...

LITTLE LOST GIRL FOUND...

So many memories...

My first memory is when I was three and a half years old, on a holiday to Trinidad with my parents. I remember it well. I guess it is because we have lots of photos. My dad's brother, Uncle Dave, had a monkey. I remember thinking how nice and strange it was to have a pet monkey. I remember family members taking me for strolls down the road, and my mum dressed me in different outfits. She is a seamstress and made all my clothes except for my underwear.

I remember my grandparents on my father's side. They remind me of traditional-looking grandparents, old, loving grandparents with kind smiles. I fell in love with them immediately.

I remember my godparents and their children were there, too, on holiday: Auntie Gem, Uncle and their daughters, Gabs and Sammy. Uncle (who was my only white uncle) climbed a curved coconut tree. Sam and Gabs played in the sea. Uncle Dave sat me on the car bonnet as I was extremely frightened of the sea—not a toe would go in without me screaming blue murder! Uncle Dave kept me company as he had a badly cut finger and couldn't swim. Auntie Gem teased me for being so scared... *memories.*

When I was around four years old, I asked my mum, who was in the kitchen, if I could go to the park. She said,

'Go ask yuh dad.' Dad was outside, working on a car, and I asked, 'Can I go to the park?'

'Yep,' he said. 'Go ask yuh mother!'

'I did, and she said to ask you. Well, I can go by myself.'

Dad said jokingly, 'Well, go nuh,' so I did!

It wasn't until mum was calling for dinner that they realised I was missing. Apparently, I had a habit of knocking on neighbours' doors and entering their homes to play, so they started searching the street. The neighbours joined with my family, looking for me. The police were eventually called, and to my parents' relief, they were told I was at the police station.

LOST & FOUND

Have you seen her?
Small, brown, always smiling, never with a frown...
Have you seen her?
Very chatty, thinks aloud, gets herself into trouble,
But I guess, at her age, it's allowed
Have you seen her?

Such a happy child, the last of five
Her siblings think she's spoilt...
Is that her fault?
At four years old, what does she know?!
Did she ask to be cute, to get all the birthday loot?
Did she ask for all the boxes under the Christmas tree, each tagged with her name?
Did you not think she'd want to be included in your game?
You left her out because?...
A spoilt brat, you say, because?...
So, she tried to entertain herself because?... because...
Her brothers and sister busy doing chores,
Li'l cute brownie had a job to do, too...
Sweep down the stairs and tear the toilet roll in twos...
(Papa say we use too much when we go to the loo!)

'Can I help?' she'd say. 'No, go away.'
'Can I play in your game?'
'No, yuh too young, go away.'

So, can yuh blame de chile for going astray? All she wanted to do was play!
Have you seen her?

'Yes, yes, madam, come this way.
She's safe and sound and chatting away.'
The door opens...
'Awwww there you are.'...
Next time, DON'T VENTURE PASS YUH FARDA'S CAR...
30-odd years later...
Have you seen her?
That li'l brown girl full of smiles,
Carefree in spirit, loves love and shares all she owns...
If you see her, greet her with a kiss, and tell her she's missed
Life is too short to stay lost; it's time to be found!

HOW DID I GET THERE?... MY FIRST HIDE & SEEK!

How on earth did I get to the police station, you wonder...

Well, we lived in Fulham (my first home). A man saw me walking by myself, asked me where I was going, and I told him the park. He said he would take me and took me straight to Hammersmith Police Station!! I actually remember sitting on the table with my legs swinging, eating a biscuit I believe was a digestive, drinking a glass of milk and wearing a bobby's hat and Mum coming through the door.

In that same house, around the same age, I took change from my mum's purse and got told off. Dad went to spank me, and I cried blue murder, ran out the living room, turned back, opened back the door, peeped my head around the door, quipped, 'Didn't hurt,' and ran up the stairs. Cheeky me, at four years old. Did my dad chase me? No. As usual, I got away with it. It was laughed off, and I was called cheeky. Something like this, my siblings would never have gotten away with, so they were never impressed.

I was troubled by spirits in that house. I used to see ghosts ALL the time. Seriously, I saw things and, one time, I heard footsteps coming up the stairs. When I ran to look, it was a pair of black shoes all by themselves – no lie. Shadows that shouldn't be there, noises that shouldn't be heard.

My siblings and I named it the most haunted house we ever lived in.

I remember dancing with my brother Curtis in that house. It was my birthday, and a girl from the street was there, helping me find my shoe. I was very happy and chatty beyond my years, indeed… *memories.*

I remember my fifth birthday in the next house we moved to, in Greenford. I wore black corduroy trousers and a white vest top with embroidery on it, and my hair was in an afro. Lots of friends were around the birthday table, and I stood on a chair to blow out the candles… *happy times.*

Our house backed onto a big open park separated by just an alleyway. The neighbours on the other side of the alleyway were two elderly sisters who had an apple tree. We took up the apples that fell into the alley, and Mum made the best pies.

My older brothers cut out a piece of the fence between our alley and the park so we didn't have to walk all the way around to get in. We could go straight from our back garden.

One time, two little white boys came in the bushes with me. We used to play hide and seek. Well, on that day, they were seeking something else. They turned around and said, 'We'll show you ours, and you show us yours.'

Well, I just said, 'Yeah, okay,' as I had no idea what they were on about. I think they started lifting up their tops, and as soon as I saw their hands head towards their trouser buttons, I panicked as I realised they were about to drop their pants, and I turned and ran for my life in a sweat. I'm sure I was about six or seven years old, and they were around the same age. Frightened the life outta me.

HIDE & SEEK

'Show me, show me, go on, yuh know me!
Don't freeze, don't hide, don't run
Take my hand and let me feel how God created you different from me.
I want to see if you look the same as what I saw in my dad's magazine!'
'Get away from me,
I will remain clean
I thought you were my friend,
But yuh so mean
Run, me, go run far from this crime scene.'

Forever, my life has mentally played that game
Hide and seek, hiding the pain, hiding the shame
Continually seeking identity… What's my name?
Hiding from men seeking to make me insane
Seeking restoration, time to take off the mask
She shouts 'HALLELUJAH!'
Hallelujah? What's that? You ask…
(Sssssh! I'll let you into a secret; no more hiding from the past)
For, one day, you will seek and find the Saviour, and you will be free at last.

Chapter 2

EARS THAT HEARD AND EYES THAT SAW

So, a beloved part of my childhood was definitely spent in our home in Greenford. They were days of joy and innocence (except for the episode with the two little boys in the park bushes).

Memories of aunties, uncles and cousins coming over (the majority not blood-related) but nevertheless, family to us. Sounds of laughter and excited chatter from the sitting room and children playing or just hanging out in the dining room. No cares or fears. We went out to play with freedom. I cannot remember the winter months at that time of my life. I remember thick fog. I used to think it was the clouds that had fallen down from the sky, as it was so thick and fluffy.

I remember one Christmas Eve, sleeping with one eye open, waiting for that fat, white-bearded man to come and nibble on the mince pie and juice left out for him and wonder what he'd bring me. Well, I was five years old and considered to be a good girl even though I was told I was cheeky. My eyes were failing me. Sleep beckoned, but just then, in the corner of my half-closed eye, I saw a shadow.

I jumped, sat up on my bed and rubbed my eyes so I could see properly. My feet felt something hard, and I followed my gaze, and there she was: the most beautiful Black doll you could imagine. She was the size of a 6-8-month-old baby, with short black hair, but in the middle of her head was a ponytail you could extend by pulling on the hair and make it recede by pulling on a string on her back. I was gleeful, then I remembered the shadow and ran out of my room and went downstairs; no one.

I ran into my parents' room, panting. 'Mum... Mum, Dad—Father Christmas came. I saw his shadow. He gave me a doll, a real baby—seeee?' I held up the doll in my excitement.

Mum rubbed her eyes, trying hard to play dumb and half-asleep (it worked!). She replied, 'Oh, that's real nice. Now, go to sleep.'

Sleep?

Sleep—how could I sleep? I was overwhelmed. Father Christmas had found me and brought me the best doll ever, and I named her Chrissy. I was convinced, at five years old, that there WAS a Father Christmas, and he loved me enough to come all the way to my house to give me a present.

'I am a good girl.'

1976. The hottest summer recorded, and I was six years old. Dressed in a swimming costume, I played in the fountains of Trafalgar Square with my brothers. I do not recall my big sister being there or my brother Angus, but they must've been there, too.

In my mind, I see myself running, giggling, laughing and wet.

'I sense happiness.'

1977. The Queen's Silver Jubilee. There was red, white and blue everywhere, all over my school. I remember having to dress up like British kings and queens with large hats, having a garden party at school, watching the parade on telly and thinking how lovely the world was with so many happy people. No one said anything about my hair or my colour. No one had ever answered my question: 'Why are we not called "brown" people and white people "cream" or "coloured"?' Anyway, it was a great year, and I felt different outside of my home. I felt accepted.

My big sister Cam use to take me with her when she visited her friends.

I don't really know if she did it out of kindness or if she was made to do it as she may have been in charge of looking after me. Regardless, I loved my outings with her. Her friends were always so nice to me, and I loved the attention of being the 'baby sister'.

I don't even know when he came on the scene, but my sister had this boyfriend. I remember Mum not being happy about something then. Years later, I realised it was because my sister got pregnant.

In all of that drama, we moved house, and the next thing I knew, Mum was busy sewing, and my cousin and I had pretty dresses to wear. My other cousins came over from abroad, and there was pure excitement. Why? Because there was going to be a wedding, my sister's wedding, and she was hugely pregnant. There were lots of people, the sun shone and there were loads of food at the reception. The one thing that stood out to me was the huge bread loaf shaped like a duck.

A lot of work and money went into that wedding and a lot of stress, I imagine, but my mother (especially) did not want the 'embarrassment' of a pregnancy outside of wedlock.

Anyway, I got to be a bridesmaid for the first time ever.

For my sister, it wasn't a case of 'I do' but rather, 'I have to'!

I decided then that I wanted to get married for love.

The wedding was in June 1978, and it was the beginning of a wonderful summer. I became an auntie to a beautiful baby girl. I was nine years old and automatically felt very grown up. I remember, my mum came rushing into the house from work like a whirlwind to grab a dressing gown and slippers for my sister and rushed back out to head to the hospital. Somewhere within all the excitement was the information that Cam was in labour.

I sat on the stairs, trying to imagine what that really meant. Was the baby really going to come out down there, and if so, HOW?

I smile; I wanted to be a mother.

Between the ages of nine and ten years old, I saw quite a few 'first times' in my short life.

After Cam had given birth to my niece, my parents and I travelled to America for a summer holiday the following year I took Chrissy with me, and in my hand luggage were all of my niece's clothes, aged six months. They were now Chrissy's clothes, and she would never grow out of them.

My first time...

It was strange, as I pictured the U.S. to be in the same Technicolor as what I saw in the movies! I didn't expect it to look and feel like England, with people like me.

The shops were different. There were delis everywhere. Singing accents flowed with upbeat, excited conversations. Everyone was always in a rush.

There were so many relatives and friends that there was no need to stay in a hotel. We just stayed here and there. Everyone took to my English accent, and I was told constantly, 'Oh, my garrsssh, she's too cute!' so, of course, I felt great, I felt liked, and nobody thought I was annoying!

It was such a good feeling being accepted and liked that I thought nothing of it when, one night, I complained that I couldn't sleep, and someone said, 'Come and lay with me. I'll keep you company.'

Well, of course, I got up from where I was and went into his bed. It was a single bed and proved difficult to lie in side by side, so he suggested I lie on top of him. He said to just stay quiet and sleep would come, so I did. The talking stopped. I could not sleep for a while, though, as he kept moving slowly all the time. I just thought he was trying to get comfortable, but then I started to feel uneasy because of where the movement was touching me and the soft groans coming from him.

I decided to pretend I did not notice and began to move to go back to the other bed where I was before, but he held me and whispered, 'Shhhhhhhhhhhhhsh' close to my ears.

I froze, my eyes tightly shut and frozen. I don't remember anything else.

That was the first time.

I never thought much about what happened except for later in life when I realized that he had made me feel safe and then he had used me. Inside, I felt sick and angry. It was not rage but a coldness that curdled me from the inside and masked itself on the outside, where I still had the sweet, cute smile they all adored. I trusted no one. I hated the way he acted, as if it had been nothing. He chatted and laughed and went on with his days as normal. Was a child as small as me supposed to be able to imagine something like that? Had it all been a dream? Hell, no. It was real, it was nasty, and I hated feeling as if people were just pretending to like me so they could get close enough to hurt me. Did anyone like me? Anyone?

Lots of newfound cousins seemed to like me. I met my great uncle, who had 11 sons; they were so lovely. I met my dad's sister and family in Washington, D.C. We toured the Monument and The White House. We went to Connecticut, Baltimore, Queens, Brooklyn, just all over, and it was great. Lots of pleasant, memorable first times.

We were out visiting again. I had no idea who or where until I heard 'Sister!'

I had a sister? Where? When?

Then I get this crash course story that my dad had two daughters before he met my mum—I HAVE TWO EXTRA SISTERS!

A barrage of thoughts entered my mind. Where had they been all my life? Why was I not told about them before? Why were they some big secret? Dad lived in England with us. He had not been on holiday to America, so had he even seen them? How could he not look after them? Really? I felt so sad for my new-found sisters and bad as well because I felt it was our fault (my other sister and brothers) that Dad might not have been there for them.

Wait—I had a niece? Not Cam's daughter, but another one, an older one, from my eldest sister.

I felt robbed! All this time I thought I became an aunt for the first time the year before, when in fact I'd been an auntie for a few years and didn't even know it.

The first time I met my sister, I kept staring, I guess still in shock, and I had so many questions that I could not ask, but I desperately wanted to. My niece was hooked on *Sesame Street*, and I remember that my sister took us to the cinema to see *The Muppet Movie*. My niece called me 'Aunt Maria' and loved playing with me and my doll, Chrissy. I had so much fun with her that I forgot about the other stuff that had made me feel upset and weird. I now felt the love I wanted, untarnished, unconditional, childlike love.

That was my first time.

I started to feel negative about my dad, and a layer of respect peeled away... for the first time.

WHISPERS

You whisper gently by my ear
You tell me calmly, your touch, I should not fear
But I cringe when you come so near
Being alone with you, I will refrain
For I am much too young to have such stains
How can you, being older than me, not know what you do?
Yet you insist on bringing spiritual pain
What does it profit; tell me, what will you gain?
It's a demonic sickness within your brain
Corrupting your innermost being
Driven by an un-heavenly host
Whose plan for us all is utterly insane.
God also has a plan
If anyone can break this chain
I know, in my heart, He can
It's decreed in His word, and His word never fails
Jeremiah 29:11, I shall hold on to for it allows me to prevail
Whisper no more your egocentric lies
Pretending to love
And corrupt my innocence in an unlawful soul tie
My God, my Father, sees and has built a blood hedge to cover me
Yes, I am His daughter
I did not know it back then
I choose to remember no more
You are defeated
For as I write this
I shut the door
Shut up!

APOLOGY SELFIE!

Dear Dookie Dooks,

I'm sorry that whilst your insides were broken-hearted and you cried internally, I made you pretend and suppress your feelings, and it just rooted and grew with you. I'm sorry I didn't protect you, Dookie, but you were and still are loved very much. Please forgive me.

It is because of this, I guess, that you froze and pretended when you went on holiday, and that person invited you to come and lie down in his bed for cuddles; you thought, Yes, somebody likes me.

So, you were happy to feel their love and affection whilst on holiday. They treated you like a real kid sister, and I know you felt loved and accepted. There was a huge smile on your face when cuddling with him. Nine years old, you were, and I remember it as if it were yesterday.

You thought nothing of it.

Again, I silenced you, froze you as still as a dormouse as his body started to move underneath you. At first, you thought he was just repositioning himself to get comfortable—I know, I was there—but his circular movement and the pressing against your body—not just any part of your body, but down there, in the private area, no one was allowed to see or touch.

I know you felt uncomfortable, but you were so happy being loved and accepted that I froze you. I sealed your lips and made you pretend you didn't feel like he was doing something rude. His movements reminded you of what you might have glimpsed on telly from time to time by accident, what married people do to have babies. Your innocence wondered if that meant he loved you as a wife. Baby girl, you were nine years old and not old enough to be anyone's wife.

I'm sorry.

So, so sorry that I didn't open your mouth so you could say, 'No thanks. I like my own bed!' or speak out loud with your cheeky self and say, 'Why do you keep moving? It feels funny.' That would have alerted the others who slept in the same room.

Sorry, Dookie. I should have given you your voice when it mattered most.
Now, all I have done is make you think that people show they really like you by touching you inappropriately. It wasn't your fault. You didn't know. You just wanted to be liked and loved and to be accepted.

Please forgive me,

Yours sincerely,

Me xxx

Part 2

Teenage Years

INTRO

FAKE FRIENDS, FAKE BOYS TO MEN

Growing into teenage years
The past was set behind me
Longing for life to be kind to me
Longing to not be lonely
Lots of friends on my street
Now we play a kinder, child-friendly hide & seek
Innocence is mine again
But then...
A target I seem to have become
'Touch her, caress her, she won't say a word
A voice like hers is seldom heard.
Let's learn how to be big boys
Let's explore.'
And there, innocence lost again
I'm really beginning to hate men
Out of all the girls playing hopscotch and Double Dutch
It's me, it's me, always me they illegally touch

Sad thing is, it wasn't just strangers
Maybe that's why it hurt so much
I loved you, looked up to you, I adored you
Obviously, you, I never knew

Chapter 3

IT'S ONLY A GAME

Moving to Banks Avenue was the best. There was no park behind our garden fence, just a maze of alleyways, which soon turned into our playground. The adjoining streets met at different points, making playtime and exploring fun.

There was a vast difference between this area of Sudbury and Greenford; it was like we'd moved to another country: the Caribbean! From living on a long road where you could count the Black people on one hand to an area where you could count the white people on one hand; oh, yes—talk about culture shock! Our family lived just a two-minute walk from the main road, with all the shops you could possibly need.

Not just shops but banks, the launderette, buses and friends. Oh, my goodness, so many friends, and the same colour as me! That was so weird. There were more than

16 families on my street alone, with kids my age, and we were all friends. No longer did Mum have to find people for me to stay with in the summer holidays and half-terms. All she had to do was knock on the neighbours' doors and let them know I was home, so keep an eye out. I was 13 and capable of staying at home on my own. My sister and a couple of brothers had left home, but they came around often.

Mum had strict instructions: play outside after all my chores were finished and stay where the neighbours could see me. Everyone used to knock on each other's doors, asking to play out on the road. We played skipping, athletics, Hopscotch, blind man's bluff, roller-skating, skateboarding, cycling and 'Had', running in and out of the alleyways.

Life was good.

Mum's instructions were strict, but the number-one rule that was not to be broken was NO BOYS ALLOWED IN THE HOUSE. Mum was such a stick in the mud as that rule stood, even if she was home. I always wondered why she just didn't send me to an all-girls school.

As the younger children on the street, we had nothing to worry about, as we felt safe having the older boys around and a few older girls who looked out for us. Me and my friend Sam used to race around the block. As we approached where the older boys congregated, we always slowed down to say hello. They asked how we were, and we felt great as they remembered our names and knew where we lived. For some reason, it felt great to be remembered.

There were woods near where we lived, and a large group of us used to walk there and have loads of fun playing hide and seek and picking blackberries for Mum to make blackberry jam. There were some steep hills that we navigated down to a group of trees we etched our names on. We had fun rolling down the grassy hills and sliding down on a piece of board when it snowed heavily The air was forever filled with laughter.

Life was good.

One of the older boys showed me extra attention. I felt special and all gooey inside, but I was just a girl of 13 and thought he was just a flirt as I didn't think I was pretty enough to be girlfriend material. The day came when there was a knock on my front door whilst my mother was at work. It was the summer holidays, and I was looking after Cam's daughter. I had just come in from playing outside, and my niece was tired.

It was him.

'So, can I come in? I won't be long. Just want to chat.' He shone a smile that seemed to hypnotise common sense away from me, and I threw all caution to the wind. My niece said hello, smiled and did the biggest yawn. I said to hang on a minute, and I'll put her to lie down. I took her upstairs, and when I did, he came into the house and shut the door quietly. Coming down the stairs, I saw the door shut and thought he had gone. I walked into the living room, and there he was, sitting on the sofa, smiling, beckoning for me to come and sit down. My insides were in a panic. It was late in the day, and Mum would be home soon, in about an hour or so, and there was a BOY in the house. Oh, my gosh—I felt so clammy.

He told me to relax and that everything was okay, so I went to sit next to him, and his smile melted any anxiety I had. He came up close and kissed me, and then his hands moved up and down my body. I froze, my mind frantic, screaming inside yet frozen on the outside. Did I like it or not? I was confused, happy for the attention of a boy like him supposedly liking me, yet scared of what was taking place.

I literally zoned out and was as still as a mannequin. He continued to touch me whilst reassuring me it was okay. I couldn't say a word. I could only just about breathe. I did not realise the zipper of his trousers was down, and he'd slipped my panties to one side. He flipped me around and held me down. I was frightened—very frightened—but I was pinned.

'Ssshhhhhhh—it's okay. You can't get pregnant, and you'll still be a virgin if I do it like this.'

Dumb me!

Was he really going to do what I thought?

YES, he did.

I felt this pulsating, very warm mass going into my back passage, and I unfroze in the greatest panic. I fought my way out from underneath him and told him through my teeth, 'LEAVE ME ALONE... my niece is upstairs. What on earth would I do if she woke up to see THIS??

He smirked and said, 'I'm just playing with you. It's just games.'

He tried to grab me back, but I looked up and shouted. 'My mum's here. She's parking!!'

I was lying, but he didn't take the chance. He jumped up, fixed his trousers and ran out the back door, over the fence and down through the alley. Fifteen minutes later, Mum really did come home. I felt sick and dirty. His words lingered in the air. He was playing, and thought it was a game—so, he didn't really like me? I wasn't girlfriend material, I thought.

Who was I fooling? Someone like me? No, he used me to abuse me.

That was the start of my boiling hot baths. I ran hot baths and slowly lowered myself down into the water. I needed to be clean, and in my mind, only scalding water could help cleanse me. I also walked the four miles to school. The breeze blew on me, blowing away the dirt. My thoughts made no sense, but they made sense to me. To walk to school meant I had to walk past his house. Sometimes, he came out to head to school, saw me and laughed, asking if I came looking for him, ridiculing me. My eyes faced away in shame. I dared not let him see them well up with tears of shame and disgust. I felt so dirty every day.

If the shame and filth weren't enough, that same day, when my mum came home, when my niece awoke, she turned to look at me and smiled as she said, 'Grandma, I fell asleep when the boy came around' (she was always such a brat with me when Mum was home). What was the point of trying to explain? What could I say? All I heard was shouting. All I felt was licks. All I could do was cry. The tears were more from the dirty experience I'd endured only half an hour before. Mum beating me was null and void.

Life turned ugly and dirty.

My mum and my sister made friends with people on the opposite side of the road. The lady had a daughter the same age as my sister and two sons, who were maybe three and five years older than me. One evening, in the summer holidays, when my cousin was staying over, Mrs Agard came over to visit. Both she and Mum were in the living room, chatting away over a cup of tea. My sister was upstairs with Angela, Mrs Agard's daughter, so it was just myself, my cousin Fred and Mrs Agard's two boys, Gregory and his older brother Paul, left to entertain ourselves in the dining room. Nothing much was on TV, so we decided to play hide and seek, not that there were many places to hide. We took turns counting whilst the rest of us ran around downstairs, trying to find places to hide in the kitchen and dining room. Our giggling sometimes gave our places away. Fred wasn't a real cousin, but we called his parents Auntie and Uncle. They were close friends of Mum and Dad, so he was like a cousin to us. We were the same age, but he was two months older than me. We got on quite well. Out of the brothers, Greg was much quieter than Paul.

It was Paul's turn to count. I ran and hid under the dining table. There was a tablecloth that hung over it, nearly to the ground. Just as I knelt to crawl under it, Fred came in under it, too, and I started giggling. He was trying to tell me to be quiet, but I couldn't stop giggling, so he leaned over and put his lips over my mouth to kiss me. At that very moment, the tablecloth went up, and Paul saw Fred pull away. He gave us a tiny smirk. I think we all pretended that nothing happened. All Paul said was. 'Fred, it's your turn.'

As Fred got up to go count, Paul whispered that we should stay under the table as he surely wouldn't think to look there again. As we sat waiting, Paul pulled me closer and whispered, 'I'll show you how it's done better,' and with that, he tilted my head back, placed his lips over mines, and sensually parted them with his tongue.

I froze. I was scared yet confused. Was he saying he fancied me, or was he just teaching me how to kiss? I couldn't move, couldn't breathe. I was scared to talk, to respond. My mind had a million voices, along with alarm bells, telling me that my mum was just in the next room and the others were around.

Greg and Fred both came to find us. I felt flushed, hot and bothered, but they couldn't see that I was blushing—it's a good thing I wasn't a white girl!

Paul acted as if everything was normal. Greg fussed that he didn't want to count as he claimed Fred had cheated. To prevent a squabble and save our mums from shouting, I offered to count instead. My counting was slow as my thoughts were having their own conversation.

'Ready or not, here I come.' I went to all the possible hiding places except the table, which I passed numerous times, glancing over at it to see if I saw movement. I found Gregory under the stairs first and Fred at the side of the cupboard by the front door. As I thought, Paul was under the table. He came out and whispered, 'I saw you come in—why didn't you come to me?'

I was mute. I looked down as he took my hand and whispered, 'Find me, or I'll find you,' and he smiled.

What was that smile? What did it mean? Find him! Did he like me, then? Did he fancy me? Gosh, he was so handsome, and his eyes were a beautiful olive green, which was mesmerising. I guess it was due to his mother being a fair-skinned Jamaican lady, and his dad was the same, mixed with white, I imagined.

As Greg began to count, I pulled my hand away and ran. I broke the rules and went upstairs and into the bathroom… and there, I found Fred.

It was too late to move as Greg had stopped counting. 'Hey, you're cheating,' I whispered.

'Well, so are you. I won't tell if you let me kiss you again.'

I felt sick. I didn't like that I had turned into a kissing magnet; this wasn't 'Kiss Chase!'

'We are cousins, Freddie. You can't—shouldn't. It's not allowed. It's dirty.'

He smiled. 'Our parents just say that, but we aren't real cousins, so we can.' And before I could protest any more, he kissed me—not like Paul, not a quick peck.

Stop... stop... stop.

I couldn't breathe. My mind urged my body to move, yet I felt stuck.

I picked up the energy and ran downstairs to stop the game, but Greg had found Paul, and Paul insisted he had one more turn.

Don't ask me how I got there, but I found myself under the table. I felt like I was under a spell.

Paul turned off the light and shouted that the dining room was out as the hiding place had become too obvious... yeah, right!

The counting stopped. 'Ready or not, here I come,' and that, he did, straight under the table. He leant in and started to touch me on my chest. My heart stopped, and I gasped for air, but he shushed me and said how much he liked me and wanted me to be his girl, and this was what boyfriends and girlfriends did. He rubbed my budding chest, breathed heavily and kissed me, pushing his tongue deeper, but I gagged.

I came to my senses. It was like I had left my body for a moment and came back in. I couldn't move; I felt paralysed, but I gritted my teeth to stop his soft, warm tongue from entering again. Did that mean he loved me? It was dark, and all I felt were fingers travelling in equally dark, forbidden places on my body. I couldn't stop him. I was confused—was I supposed to like that?

'Boys, Angela, it's time to go say goodbye.' Paul crawled out, double time, and switched on the light. Fred and Greg came from upstairs, complaining that Paul took too long. His explanation was that they had gone upstairs, which wasn't allowed. I forced a smile to say goodbye to Mrs Agard and waved to the boys and their sister as I had no more words. I stared at Paul, waiting for him to lock eyes with me, seeking confirmation of his fancying me, but his eyes danced everywhere except on me.

The front door shut, and I just stood there. Fred was staying over. Mum said it was time to settle down and suggested we get ready for bed.

Lights out, and I was sharing a bed with Freddie, head to tail as we did in those days, with the door shut. In the darkness, I heard him whisper, 'We are allowed. We're not cousins. Let me kiss you. It's nice.' I looked blankly in the dark, seeing a silhouette move like a ghost as my lips sealed with his, daring not to make a noise to make Mum barge in and tell us off.

Yes, I see now—that was where my fear of the dark began. Oh, and, no, Paul paid me no more attention after that evening.

I was told we were going to Trinidad, Dad, Mum and I. The excitement I felt was because I was going to see my grandparents, whom I loved dearly. They were the typical-looking grandparents: Granddad had the whitest hair and the longest beard, and Grandma was a cute, small-framed woman. Both were very loving.

I remembered them from my holidays when I was little, and that Granddad had a church in his garden, and he was a preacher. At school, when we were in woodwork and told to think of something and make it, I had a great idea: I was going to make a Granddad a bookrack to rest his Bible on.

It was great being back in Trinidad. The smell of the humidity when the plane doors opened was just intoxicating. The drive from the airport was always early evening, so the air was always filled with cooking from the doubles stalls, restaurants and homes.

The capital is Port of Spain, and that's where we stayed... well, where we were based, as we had lots of family to visit. The day came for us to travel down south, deep into the countryside, to visit my grandparents. They were just as I remembered. I proudly presented the varnished bookrack to Granddad, and he loved it. It was the first thing I'd ever made in woodwork.

At the back of the house was land as far as my eyes could see, filled with coffee bean and cocoa trees, and it all belonged to our family. There were also chicken and duck pens (I thought they were pets!). It was quite humorous, brushing my teeth and rinsing my mouth out the window and watching the ducks and chickens run to gobble up the minty water. It was quite disgusting, actually—there was no sink! The house was a board house, made out of planks of wood, and we washed in the yard surrounded by sheets of galvanised metal. The toilet? Well, it was what they called a latrine, with galvanised metal sheets creating a little space with a boxed seat to sit on. It stunk to high heaven—I'm sure excretions from my forefathers were still in there. In the nighttime, you had to take a flashlight. As soon as the light shone in there, it came alive with movement: cockroaches, lizards, moths and other unknown insects scarpered everywhere.

That was it for me. As big as I was, I used the bedpan to urinate, and Mum or Dad took it outside to empty it. For love or for money, I wasn't entering there again. My stomach froze with any bowel movements, and I didn't go for a week.

Sunday was the best day, as Sunday dinner was like Christmas dinner, and my grandma had the sweetest hand when it came to seasoning and cooking. She asked me what I'd like for dinner, and I said chicken. Grandma said, 'Chicken, it is.'

I looked forward to going to the supermarket with her as I hoped to get some rhubarb sweets.

I waited and waited, so I went to see what was taking Gran so long to get ready. There she was, in the chicken pen with a long cutlass in her hand. She grabbed a chicken and put it on the scale. Obviously not pleased, she let it go and caught another one. She came out of the pen, and I was still clueless as to what was about to happen. I just thought it all comical. Then, the bucket was over the body of the chicken with its head and neck sticking out, and before I could think my next thought, the cutlass came swiftly down, and there was a bloody, headless chicken running aimlessly around the yard. Well, I screamed with my mouth open for the longest while, catching flies.

'Grandma, why did you do that? Whyyyy?'

She laughed at me and said, 'But is you who tell me yuh want chicken.'

'Well, I didn't mean for you to kill one of your pets. I thought we were going to the shops.'

Gran replied, still chuckling, 'So where the chicken come from in the supermarket?!' What a revelation that was.

I watched Grandma soak it, pluck it, wash it down with lemon and season it with fresh herbs and spices. The smell soon made me forget the trauma for a while. Her cooking smelt so delicious; I was so hungry and couldn't wait.

Dinner was ready, and I was told to find Granddad and tell him. I looked everywhere. Finally, I found him in his little church. I looked everywhere. Finally, I found him in his little church, with a woman who was lying on top of a table on her back... naked. It felt so wrong. I couldn't move.

I couldn't move.

He was dressed in a white robe and rubbing her down. He must've sensed me there and came out from behind a see-through curtain, which resembled a mosquito net.

I mumbled in a low voice, 'Grandma says dinner is ready.'

'Thank you. Don't be frightened—I'm just giving this lady a spiritual bath to cleanse her.' Well, I guess that made sense: she was naked, and he was a preacher, and he smelled of fragrant oils.

'Come and give Granddad a kiss.' He held his arms out.

I smiled and walked towards him. I just loved my Grandddad and didn't question what he said. He leaned towards me. Thinking he was going to kiss my cheek, I raised my head up. He went to my mouth and stuck his huge tongue in it and twiddled it around.

I nearly jumped out of my skin and ran out of the church for dear life. I could hear him calling out, 'It was just a game. Grandpa only playin', chile,' in his strong Trinidadian accent.

Playing? What the heck, GRANDDAD!!!! MY BELOVED GRANDAD.

My world crashed. The feeling has stayed in my mouth even to this day.

I went under the house—it was built on stilts—sat on the bench, held in my tears and rocked with my arms wrapped around me, squeezing in the sounds of my innermost sobbing. Who would I tell? Who would believe me? My happiness left me forever, I would never smile again. God's eyes hadn't seen this little sparrow. He wasn't watching over me. The song in my spirit fell silent. I was alone. How many times must other people's tongues be in my mouth? What kind of love was that?

I sat at dinner, my appetite gone, and just played with my food. The trouble was that Mum was a stickler when it came to children eating up all of their food; she hated waste. Darling Grandma stuck up for me and said she'd given me too much and to leave 'de chile' alone.

Granddad approached when we were eating, and I quickly asked to be excused. How could I ever love him again? Thankfully, we were to leave the next day. I couldn't face him again.

As we got ready to leave, my parents kept prodding me to go give Granddad a hug and a kiss goodbye. They couldn't understand why, all of a sudden, my countenance had changed. Reluctantly, I gave him the quickest hug and said bye. I explained that I just felt unwell. Thankfully, Mum put it down to my not having opened my bowels for just over a week. Thank God. My grandma joked that she promised to build a proper toilet just for me by the time I came back to visit. That made me smile, but the last thing I wanted was to come back.

Life was not good. At 13 years old, it was dark, horrid, ugly, filthy and lonely.

HUSH NOW...

Hush li'l grandchild
Don't say a word
You found Grandpa
but no sounds could be heard
Images flooded your eyes and mind
Surely, this was not what you expected to find
Silent questions with answers that made no sense
You stand in the church; nausea grows intense
There's a sweet aroma of an unusual incense
The one you least expected has again broken your innocence.
Who is friend, who is foe?
Baby girl, back then, not even I did know
Being frozen has become habitual
You lock off to reality
To shut off the brutality
Of the obscene works of profanity
Questioning your virginity
Hush, my li'l Dookie
For I am to blame
Again, I didn't protect you
I'm so sorry; I feel ashamed
I am you, and you are me
Trying so hard not to induce in you fear
That freezes you, so all you can do is cry out with flowing tears
You are loved, I promise
A love that is pure and real
In years to come, you will realise it's Jesus Christ

Until then, dry your eyes
Block out their illegal touch
Hush now, most beautiful Dookie, as it's all too much.
Hush now.
Please forgive me.
Yours sincerely
Me!

Chapter 4

THE HIGHS & LOWS OF HIGH SCHOOL

A few years passed, and things settled down. I still had hot baths, still went for long walks and still hated the dark.

High school was okay, I guess. I had friends, but I wasn't with the 'in crowd', so I felt unnoticed, which was a good thing as I got my work done and had good reports. Back then, our school system was Year 1–5, then sixth form. By the time I reached Year 4, I had started to break out of my shell a bit. I was tired of being overlooked. My friends smoked in the toilets, and I was the lookout person in case the dinner ladies or teachers on patrol came around until one of the girls had a barney and insisted I take a puff, as she thought that if I didn't,

I'd snitch on them. So, I reluctantly started smoking at age 14; sad but true.

Nearly everyone had a boyfriend or a girlfriend, but I wasn't sure I wanted one. I thought that maybe it was a chance to cover up the past by having someone to like me the way I wanted to be liked. My friends giggled and teased that Shaun Tate fancied me and wanted to ask me out. Shaun was nice-looking, quiet, and he was part of the in-crowd. He was my golden ticket to being noticed.

Well, Shaun Tate asked me out. Back in my day, going out meant that you hung around together at break times and walked home together, and at the odd cinema if you lied to your parents that you were going out with Suzi down the road! No one ever went out—with what money? With whose permission?

Shaun walked me a few stops down from my usual bus stop so we could talk for a while together. There was a day we walked through the park, and it was a bit chilly. In fact, it was very chilly. We stopped by a bench farther into the park and sat down. There was this awkward silence, and then he leaned over to kiss me.

Shaun Tate kissed ME.

He put his hands on my shoulders and kissed me again. He was very gentle, yet I could tell he was nervous as hell. Maybe it was his first time, as it became sloppy.

We kissed again, this time with our mouths open and our tongues out—huge yuk! Oh, my goodness—I felt his saliva run down the side of my mouth. My first real consensual kiss, and it was DISGUSTING. That was the first and last time we kissed; we broke up soon after that.

I started to bunk classes and wrote notes forging my mum's signature. I never left the school grounds; I just spent loads of time smoking in the girls' toilets. My character was changing, and the teachers started to notice I was getting a little cheeky. One time, I went too far. I was walking down the corridor with my chain hanging out of my shirt. My R.E. teacher saw me and said to put my chain inside my shirt. I cheekily and disrespectfully answered, 'What's your problem? It's got a cross on it, hasn't it?'

Well, who told me to say that?! Mum was called for a meeting down at the school. Dad never came; he never did.

Lord, have mercy on my soul! A lot of my friends' parents charged at the school like bulls to have a go at the teachers or the kids themselves, who troubled their little angels, but not my Grenadian/Trinidadian ole-school strict Mum, who believed wholeheartedly in 'don't spare the rod'. My Mum would not think twice about beating me in front of the whole school.

The day came, and I was told to go fetch my mum from reception. She was breathing with flared nostrils. Out of five children, I was the only one she had to be called to the school for. I walked five steps in front of her all the way to Sir's office and sat down, trying to find all the excuses to talk away all the problems I'd created.

Sir was really nice, though. He said they'd noticed a change in my behaviour and were concerned that I'd changed my friends for the worst, and my attitude was becoming like them. Sir emptied out an envelope with all of these documents—my documents—inside. They'd kept all of my little notes—what the heck? I thought they'd read them and thrown them away.

I glimpsed at the signatures, and for the first time, I realised how majorly fake they looked. I just sat there, praying for God to help me and not to let my mum notice. He really does love me as she noticed not one. Never again was I cheeky. There was no way I would do anything for my mum to come down to the school again unless it was for Parents' Evening!

Fifth year was the last year of high school unless you were a geek and stayed on to sixth form. There were a few subjects that I liked: Social Studies, English, German and Home Economics. R.E. was annoying as we studied every other religion in depth other than Christianity.

Now, Miss Know-it-all as I was, I had my heart set on becoming a top chef. All I needed was to know how to cook, and my mum was teaching me well. R.E. was of no use; Social Studies was of no use, and as for Maths—was I really going to go into a shop and ask for two square roots of bananas?

Dear Mr Pratt was our maths teacher. Looking back, I realised that he was young but so obese that he was such an easy target to take the mick out of and stress him out in class.

I was hopeless at times tables that didn't have a pattern for easy learning. Long division was truly long, and equations and fractions and those silly symbols and using letters for numbers made no sense. What did make sense, though, was sitting at the back of the class and spending the lesson with rounds of blackjack, the greatest card game. I roped in a couple of players at a time, taking turns playing one-on-one. Due to the layout of the desks, we couldn't have any more players.

That was the only thing that made us look forward to Maths. The odd time we would get caught by Pratt, my cocky answer was, 'It's numbers, ennit?' He advised once, he advised twice, and then he told me that one day, I would amount to nothing and with that, he never bothered me again. Who cared? I didn't. Chefs didn't need maths! Oh, boy.

The final weeks of the end of school were approaching, and the excitement was building for the annual fifth-year disco. Then, they hit us one morning in assembly: 'You are, by far, the worst year group we have taught and undeserving of an end-of-year disco.'

No disco? No disco! No way. So, a few of us banded together to plan our own party in the sixth form common room during lunch hour.

Everyone in was to buy or bring a bottle from home. I covered my back to a point—I told Mum that we were having an end-of-year party (obviously run by the school!), and I needed to bring a drink. I explained that the teachers said we were allowed Babycham as it was a special occasion. My mum fell for it as Babycham was considered a light drink, suitable for children, and I was always allowed it at family parties.

During the morning break, we took off our blazers and school ties and went down to the Triangle Off Licence. Looking back, I have no idea how we thought we looked old enough to buy alcohol or even how the shop attendant served us.

At the end of our lesson, I advised (like I'm a big-time drinker), 'Don't drink on an empty stomach. Make sure to eat something and drink milk to line the stomach so as not to get sick.' Well, that's what I thought to be correct.

The sixth form common room was buzzin', blackjack in one corner and drinks and laughter in the next. No one had any idea how to handle themselves; they just drank for drinking's sake. There was Thunderbird, which was a strong wine, Babycham, Captain Morgan rum, Tenents and Special Brew beer.

Against my advice, they drank them all, a cocktail brewing in their bellies. The next thing I knew, most of my mates were legless. By the time we went to our next lesson, we were, as they said back then, 'carked'.

I was in maths, sitting at the back of class. There was no blackjack; I was just trying to keep a clear head. All of a sudden, the door flung open, and our head of year stormed in without explanation. He stood there, his eyes scanning the room. His eyes finally settled on me, and he pointed a finger at me and Len and said 'YOU! YOU. OUTSIDE. MY OFFICE. NOW!'

The task before me was to stand up and walk in a straight line, I was really shaky, but I had to keep steady so I could play things down.

I managed to walk past him, as he stood there, talking sternly to the rest of the class, asking who else was involved in the binge... Oh, my gosh! How did he know?

As soon as I walked past him, I skedaddled down to his office. I had to get a clean distance so he couldn't see me swagger.

To get to Sir's office, I had to pass the medical room, and there was the reason: Jenna and Waverley were sitting there with their heads in buckets, bringing up cocktails! I was so mad. Man, I'd told them to line their stomachs and take it easy so as not to get drunk. I sobered up immediately.

I was questioned intensely, but I kept it together. I told Sir we just wanted to celebrate and ONLY had Babycham!!! I explained that even my Mum had said that a little Babycham was okay, but I didn't realise you could get tipsy on it.

He bought it! Then, he hit me with a bombshell: he had already rang my mum, and she was on her way to pick me up as I wasn't allowed in school under the influence of alcohol.

There was just one more problem: I had told Sir that we'd only had Babycham, yet a flashback reminded me of the bottles and cans of alcohol we'd thrown down the toilets. After he dismissed me to collect my school bag,

I ran down to the common room, grabbed a plastic bag from the bin and picked those damn bottles and cans out of the toilets (wasn't so funny now!). I carried them off the school grounds before my mum got there and put them in a public street bin. That was a close call.

My mum drove up, nostrils flared, eyes bulging, and I was like, where and how could I run? Praise God, my darling Uncle Ken was with her, and he kept saying, 'Eli, leave de chile alone nuh,' in his soft Trini accent. 'She dun get boof up by she teacher and sent home. She'll not do this again.'

Mum sighed and told me sharply to get in the car. I jumped in so fast, just in case she changed her mind at the last minute and to beat me in public.

Waverley and Jen were off from school for a good few days. After it all blew over, we laughed about it and still do to this present day.

Exams were excruciating. The only date in history I could remember was the Battle of Hastings, 1066. I got okayish grades, but the worst was maths—are you surprised?! I remember, on exam day, I wrote my name, form and date on the front page, turned over the page and stared at gobbledegook, I turned the page back over and sat there in silence until everyone had finished. Blackjack had gotten me a C.S.E. grade of a 'U', the lowest possible mark, meaning 'ungraded'.

My best grades were in Home Economics, of course.

That was it for me; no more high school.

Alison Ryan -Chase

SCHOOL BELL RINGS...IT'S OVER

Algebra History
Maths and boring, irrelevant stories
Why must I know the exact date?
Whatever happened happened, I can't change it; it's too late!
Don't tell me that
Treating me like I'm inadequate
I know I played when I should have paid attention
But I just couldn't see how maths came into the equation
As you taught the class, my counterparts, in turn, whispered 'pass'
And so it was I became the maths class champion of a pack of 52
Refusing to adhere to school rules
Closing my ears so as not to listen to you
Teachers screaming down the corridors
Children being a nuisance and slamming doors
Smoking in the toilets
Escaping the unrevised class tests
Wondering do we have to really do our best?
For the teachers already decided which set we'll be in
School sucks, I thought, and was like the rubbish in the rubbish bin
Supposed to be the best years of our lives
But the playground always had a fight
The classrooms a battle with teachers' strife
I sit and wonder, 'What the hell?'
And wait patiently for the bell
I realised a little too late
When I, for the last time, walked out the school gate
That the teachers I thought were full of hate

Were the ones who were right. It was me who couldn't relate
Now, it's the end of year five
My exam results just made me want to hide
I wish I'd stuck to being teacher's pet
To be a good girl and have the world on my plate
If only I could turn back time
Do good in maths and not step out of line
Why did I feel the need to fit in so?
Where are those friends now that it's time to go?
College, uni, in good jobs
You see, the bad crowd were loud for all to see
But behind closed doors, they studied and learnt well
They made out it was cool to be dumb
And all the time they were competing to be number one
Looking at them, I could not tell
Lower and lower my grades fell
This did not stop me from reaching high
I got up and tried my hardest
Finally taking responsibility and exploring the depths of my capabilities
Stretching my brain cells to the farthest
You see...
It IS in you, and it IS in me
God made us intelligent
Don't follow the crowd
Just be you, and you'll see how much can be achieved.
Stay close to your teachers, trust and believe
They'll help and guide you so exams will be stress-free
And your grades will be worth something by the time you leave.

Chapter 5

KILBURN POLY'S BLACKJACK PUNISHMENT!

I got in! I was a college student and not with the weirdos in sixth form.

Our first day was super cool. We sat in pairs and listened to the introductions, what to expect and what the lecturers, not the teachers, but the lectures—expected of us. I couldn't contain my excitement; it was so surreal. I sat next to this other Black girl. We shared a joke, and that was it; I knew we would be friends.

Practical lessons were a breeze. I felt, at times, that I could teach *them* a thing or two!

I looked forward to our breaks as we always headed down to the cafeteria. It buzzed with an atmosphere of fun, and all the stresses of the theory lessons were discarded there.

Over to the side of the cafeteria was a table surrounded by some guys shouting and laughing. Me and my new friend Bernel were intrigued and we peeked. To my delight, they were playing a card game — yes, my beloved blackjack. Anyone could join in after someone was knocked out.

I couldn't resist. The addiction to the game was real. Bernel was a real goody-two-shoes. She was mad but not as mad as me. She knew when to quit and head to lessons when our break was over.

Our college was a short bus ride away from Brent Cross Shopping Centre, so when the cafeteria wasn't buzzing, Bernel and I took a trip for one thing only: an Almondine! It was a sort of Danish pastry filled with sweet almond paste. It was simply out of this world delicious, especially when the attendants warmed it for us. Our lunch break was an hour; it took us 20 minutes each way to travel to Brent Cross, so we literally had to run in and run out to get back for afternoon lectures or practicals.

I was getting distracted. Bernel tried her best to get me not to skive off classes, but I was getting attention. The boys in the cafeteria liked my company, and I liked theirs. A couple of times, my eyes met with this guy Gary's. I had a feeling he wanted to ask me out. I liked that feeling. Somebody wanted me to be their girl — who would want to go to class??

I attended enough to know and understand the topics. The voice of Mr Pratt haunted me in my head:

'You won't amount to nothing.' I had to beat the feeling that he might be right.

For crying out loud, I chose to do German at school as French seemed to have so many rules on how to speak to whom. German, to me, was like broken English, and the translation was easier. Why didn't anyone tell me that French is widely used in the catering industry? I also told my maths teacher that his lessons were a waste of time, as I wouldn't go into a shop and ask for two square roots of bananas, please! So, I played blackjack instead. It was a huge mistake: weighing, measuring, conversion tables, degrees in Celsius and Fahrenheit, portion control, costing, altering ingredients for different sizes and numbers—maths, maths, maths. It was a painful revelation. So, knowing I had a stress release via the cafeteria was welcome. It seemed like a punishment for playing blackjack in Maths lessons, and it haunted me. Now, playing blackjack became my comfort zone in college, but I had no idea how to break the habit.

Gary asked me out. We were an item, but we didn't actually go anywhere except to his house when no one was home and to his bedroom—well, that's where he hung out with his friends, or so he said. We'd snuggle up, talk, giggle, and then kiss. The kisses spoke a thousand words. They were nice words, and I slipped into my fantasy world, blocking out the voices that shouted, 'NO, that's dirty. Don't let him touch you. It's wrong.' Well, I just wanted it to be right for once, to be clean and okay.

I struggled with Gary's mouth over mine. My insides shook with panic as flashbacks of similar touches from the wrong people at the wrong age alit in my mind.

'Stop, Gary. I heard something. Someone's downstairs.'

He shot up to check, and as he did, I jumped up to fix my clothes. By the time he'd turned around, I was properly dressed, with my shoes on. That relationship lasted only a few weeks. I'd let him get intimate, then I'd hate myself and freeze.

What can I say? We drifted. I stopped being like a 'girlfriend' and just played the role of a friend. He got the message.

A few weeks later, I went to a house party with my sister. There, I was dancing to some rare groove and Studio One music. The vibe was nice. It lasted late into the morning hours, and the DJ started to play 'Lovers Rock', and this guy touched my arm to dance. Of course, I felt sweet. My sister, being 10 years older than me, had friends who were more mature, and I started to prefer older guys.

Rodney was his name. We slow-danced till the pace made it look as if we weren't moving. It was a dance that told me he was going to ask for my number; and he did. Of course, I gave it to him.

Of course, I gave it to him.

Rodney and I dated for a few weeks—well, to me, going with a guy, was called dating. We didn't go anywhere on dates. It was always a case of sneaking him into my house when everyone was out. It was over three weeks, and I was getting bored. I'd been with him far too long.

It came time for me to ditch him, but he wasn't like the others. He wouldn't take no for an answer. I tried everything, said mean things to put him off me, but he was hooked and became like a stalker. I couldn't go for help as he was a secret. I mean, how could I tell my friends I'd been going out and sleeping with some guy eight years older than me? It just wasn't the look.

He came around to my house. I looked through the spy hole and refused to let him in, but he started to create a scene outside and wouldn't go away, so I had no choice but to open my door.

He looked distressed, pleading with me not to break up with him. The more he pleaded, the more he disgusted me, this big, grown man whimpering like a wounded dog. He then went too far: he said he'd kill himself, or he would refuse to leave by the time my mum got home from work.

My mum? Him? No way in hell.

I was fuming. Threaten me in my own house?

Time was ticking, and I needed him out. I told him straight that he'd lost me for good with this little stunt, and if my mum came home and saw him there, I would swear he'd forced his way in and held me hostage. I also told him that if he felt he needed to kill himself, then go right ahead, as I couldn't care less. All he'd done by coming to my house was to make me lose respect for him and hate him.

It actually worked. He left.

I shut the door hard behind him and breathed. Never again would I to let anyone know where I lived.

First-year exams were approaching, and I couldn't let men or blackjack stop me from proving my teachers wrong. I was going to do this; this was war.

I put my head down and got serious. I tried my best to be in the cafeteria only at break times — man, that was hard. It wasn't just about cooking; the practicals were straightforward — I had to concentrate on my theory.

Well, I did it. Not only did I pass in every category of the exams, I also passed with distinction.

It was time to make a visit to school!

I was on a high, so happy that I could at least make my mum relax to know that I had made the right decision in leaving sixth form to go to college. A grade like 'distinction' and 'good pass' would definitely have her overlook the terrible letter of a 'U' on my C.S.E. maths paper.

I turned up at my high school well-dressed, my first-year certificate in hand. There were a few essential subject teachers I had to see: R.E., history (as Miss Harper had always been nice to me), home economics and maths, Mr Pratt, more so to show him that I DID do well and also to apologise and admit he was right: I did need maths.

I ended up giving his maths class a sort of lecture, letting them know that trying to fit in and hanging with the cool crowd was actually what caused me to fail maths.

I explained what I thought about maths and realised too late how it related to the real world, that I thought being a chef was just about cooking and had no idea how much maths was a key part. They attentively listened as I continued. Afterwards, I advised them that the only way forward was to just get on with it, learn well, listen and do their best in exams as it was a rough world out there. I felt so good.

Mr Pratt smiled and said, 'I knew you were a good girl at heart. Well done, and keep up the good work.'

No longer did I hear their negative voices telling me what I wouldn't be. Instead, I felt rather important, grown up. I'd been asked to speak to a class—wow, me!— and I really think I made a difference. Well, I hope I did.

Seeing Mr Pratt made me feel even more confident about going to seethe other teachers. My R.E. teacher had no hope for me either I just had to find her. I found her in the staff room and called over to her, she was shocked to see me. There she was, in the staff room. I called over to her, and she was shocked to see me. Miss got up and came over with such a smug look on her face that I was about to wipe off. 'Maria, what brings you here today? Needing a reference for work?'

That was it. The doorway was open for me to score a knockout. 'No, actually. I go to full-time college and got a distinction and "good pass" in my first year. I came to let Miss Gardner know as I'm studying City & Guilds 706 1/2 Cooking for the Catering Industry.' Oh, the grin that grew on my face was likely immeasurable.

'Well, imagine that. Who would've thought? Ay, good for you. I secretly knew you had it in you. You just needed to dig deep and find it for yourself. I hope this means you have chosen your friends much more wisely than you did in high school. I must say I am proud of your success. Keep it up.'

'Thank you, Miss.' With that, I said goodbye and walked away with my eyes wide open in disbelief—had I just heard right?

My goodness. The two teachers I was cheeky to the most, the two who had told me that if I continued on my path, I would amount to nothing... their words had stung back then, and I guess that's what pushed me into not being who they said I'd be, but to be who I knew I was. I was bright, creative, polite, kind, eager to learn and do well, and they had known it all along.

Wow, they really had believed in me. Maybe it was I who needed to believe in myself, that without trying to fit in with 'the crowd', I could be anything I wanted to be.

CONTINGENCY CONSISTENCY

Oh, my goodness
Can it be?
I am the queen of blackjack
And it sets me free.
Drowning out the voices of the past
Voices that said in education, I would not last
Telling me my life was a waste with an empty head
So, what was the point then?
Why was I born? I should be dead.
Teachers had no idea
Neither did I. In some ways, I didn't care…
Yes, I did
I wanted to prove I could be loved
But those guys I was with made me…
And made me see
That real love just seemed not to be attached to me
Keep them keen, but treat them mean
That way, I give them no time to affect me
Voices of high school that followed me
Stalking me like the Grim Reaper
Waiting for me to fail my exam paper
Literacy, language barriers and numeracy
I needed to attend classes consistently.
Focus and psychologically tell myself I had a purpose
And there you have it…
I did it…
Passed with a distinction

Amount to nothing, they said
Now, I can dig a hole and put those dead voices to rest
Look ahead, my soul tells my head
Yes, I am walking in the right direction
The teachers who first caused a negative affliction
Smile as they see a less rebellious me
They patted me on the back and said they were proud of my results
In a moment, I forget all their past insults
The plan now is to study hard against all possible contingencies
Which means I must behave and attend classes with consistency
So I can receive all that's in my ordained destiny.

Chapter 6

IS THIS LOVE THAT I'M FEELIN'?

The new term began, and with that came new changes. We were no longer based in Kilburn, but in an old building called Dollis Hill House, situated on Dollis Hill. It was nowhere near Kilburn Poly so I couldn't slip out for a quick round of blackjack between classes. This was, indeed, going to be a very difficult year.

Dollis Hill House — the name was fitting as the house was literally on a hill, surrounded by houses with no shops and no fast-food joints; we were stuck. I was stuck. It was a year that was truly about getting serious. Our tutorial kitchen was huge, with many workstations, individual cookers and cupboards with pots, pans and utensils. It was very professional, and I can't lie, it made me feel very prestigious, like I was on my way to becoming a big-time chef. I was on my way to being somebody. Not just anybody: somebody.

Our year group quickly settled into our new surroundings and put our heads down as we were taught technical skills in the culinary arts. All of the basic cooking skills in year one had equipped us for this next stage; things were about to get interesting.

To my surprise, Bernel's mother worked in the students' cafeteria, and she made the best food, from Jamaican patties and English pies to Cornish pasties; it was all so tasty. She was funny, too, with her unique sarcasm, and she had a hearty laugh that cheered you up on dull days.

Our timetable allowed for long periods of free time, which I didn›t expect but was very grateful for. Bernel took me to her old high school, where some of her best friends were studying in sixth form. I had lost touch with all mine except for one, Jane Wilcock.

Bernel's friends were super cool. There were twin brothers, Saul and Patrick Clackston, and her best friends, Toni Jacobs and Kacee Rogers. It didn't take long for me to be a part of the group. After all, I was the outside girl coming in. The jokes, the laughter—I fell in love with them all. I got on especially well with Saul. We kinda clicked, and our eyes always caught each other's and that made us blush. Being no fool, Berns saw the connection and, one day, pulled me aside for a little, itty bitty chat. She knew my track record, and Saul was like her brother, so there was no way in hell she wanted him to be hurt and/or used by me. I reassured her that I liked him and I wouldn't do anything bad (not intentionally). Anyway, Saul and I talked, but nothing was really going on.

There were two days when we had had classes at Kilburn Poly. I was upstairs when Bernel entered the room and said that Saul was downstairs in the lobby to see me—me, and not Bernel. Wow. My heart started to skip. I felt good. I felt special. He wasn't like the other guys I had been with. He seemed genuine, kind, respectful, interested in me and not necessarily my body. I loved being in his company. I smiled at everything he said, even if it wasn't meant to be funny.

I went down to the lobby, and there he was, with the sweetest smile. He asked if we could talk outside. Not sure what to expect, I agreed and went outside with him.

He stood at the side of the stairs, looking at me for what seemed like ages before saying, 'I've come to ask if you'd go out with me. If you'd be my girl.' In my imagination, my legs turned to jelly, and I swayed as if I were a wave on the shores of the Caribbean Sea! I tried my hardest to look cool, holding in my extended grin and managing a decent enough smile as I said yes.

I had pep in my step. I smiled all the time. Saul was so mature, even though he was just a year older than me, and he spoke about stuff that was interesting. My mum was a seamstress and literally made all of my clothes. Saul was my greatest fan. He loved fashion and was very particular about how we dressed. Every time we went out, we would be 'the couple', best dressed in our own fashion. It wasn't until Bernel made a joke about things still going well with Saul that I realised we had been going out for over four weeks—four! And the biggest shock was that we hadn't even had sex yet. Everything about that relationship was strange, different, special. It was real. I was a grown-up teenager. Not abused by him, not used. I knew he liked me a lot; however, I'm not sure if it was love. I mean, what *was* love? All the boys and men I'd been with or who had had me—wasn't that love? And if it was, then why hadn't Saul done to me what they had? Yet he treated me as I he treated me as I imagined he would if he really loved me. I was confused.

College was going well, and I engaged in most of the lessons. I always struggled with the theory, but I was better at it than I was at school. Our weeks and months were much the same: studying, hanging out, chilling with friends. I had a bestie outside of the group, my cousin Shantel. Shantel lived in East London, and we were in each other's houses nearly every weekend, mostly me at hers. Our parents, well, our mums, allowed us to go out on a Friday or Saturday night, but at a price. No matter what time we got in, we were awoken early in the morning to clean on Saturdays or cook dinner on Sundays.

There were times we joined together with Bernel, Toni, Kacee, Patrick and Saul. Going out as a group was a blast, but over time, I began to resent it all. Why? Well, it was the only time Saul and I went out!

Months turned into a year. I couldn't believe it. One year with the same guy, not swayed by another. I was in love, wasn't I? I had a great relationship with Saul's parents, brother and extended family. I had become part of their family, and I think that's what I loved: I belonged.

I went to his house often and stayed for dinner. Saul loved cooking and often started cooking whilst his mum travelled home from work. There were times he came over to mine along with the rest of the troop. To be honest, there was no way I would feel comfortable if it were just him and me at my house, though Mum really liked Saul and his parents, and they were invited to my mum and dad's random house parties all the time. If there was one thing my parents could do, it was hold the best of the best house parties.

My dad was neither here nor there when it came to Saul. I had grown to dislike my dad anyway—since learning about my two sisters, our relationship had been made up of two words: 'Morning' and 'Night'!

Seriously, though, as much as it annoyed me, it made no sense that any one of my friends, let alone a boyfriend, would come over to mine as we weren't allowed to be in my bedroom. Our house had a through-lounge, so there was no privacy just to chill, share jokes and be ourselves. At Saul's, we were allowed to chill in his bedroom. It was so much fun, and we talked for ages about anything and everything, and that, I guess, was the glitch. It was as if we were just best friends. The only thing that made us seem different from the rest was that we held hands; he put his arm around me when we walked, and we kissed on the lips. Literally no intimacy, no tongue in the cheek, just an extended, long peck on the lips. However it did feel awesome. I felt special and warm. In the past, that was just the starters, but now it was the three-course meal in one! I hated the way men and boys had treated me in the past, but shamefully, I missed it. I missed their touch as it meant that I was desired, attractive. I just didn't understand this new type of love, and I was getting fed up, bored. My last couple of boyfriends (if I could call them that) had cars. At least we went out ON OUR OWN—you know: parties, clubs, wine bars—all undercover, hiding from my mum. I was in a safe place with Saul—too safe. Was that what married life would be like?

Saul and I started to have little arguments about silly things, but I was starting to be resentful. Deep down, I liked the parties I went to with my older brothers and sister. I'd started going out with them when I turned 18, and they allowed me to tag along. Mixing with their friends was so much cooler.

I realised what my problem was: immaturity! Hanging with guys my own age did not cut it with me. They were not mature enough, and most of them did not drive—Lord, how I missed riding in a car to go out on a date or being picked up or dropped off. Oh, and I smoked. Saul didn't, and I always felt bad about that. Truth be known, it was weird not having more intimacy. I was grateful, I guess, that I was left alone, yet my body cried out to be touched. . I became angry with myself, which was confusing even to me., and I didn't know why.

It was Saturday, and once again, there were bad feelings between me and Saul. Heaven knows what the difference of opinion was that time. I just remember us being snappy and sarcastic and leaving his house VEXED. I felt so trapped. To break up with him would be like breaking up with his whole family, and I hated the thought that everyone would think I was at fault. I mean, what was the matter with me? Why could I not be satisfied with a simple, routine peck on the lips? After all, we were only 18.

Hot tears fell from my eyes as I walked the long, winding road towards the bus stop. WHY did I feel like that? I couldn't put a finger on just one thing as it was a multitude of small things that made the HUGE thing. I was tired; I wasn't Saul's girlfriend—I was his best friend!

I was in no mood to go home for Mum to demand housework of me. Being on my own was not an option, as I would only sit and cry. There was no point going to Bernel's—Saul was one of her best friends. Her voice had rung in my ears from the very beginning: 'Don't hurt him.'

There was no point talking to Toni or Kacee as even though we had grown to be close, I still saw them as Bernel's friends, first and foremost. How could I possibly say I was falling out of love with their golden boy?

Great.

I stopped at a call box and called my sister Cam. Though she heard how fed up I sounded, her upbeat conversation just did not cut it. However, she didn't give up. In the end, she talked me into going out that evening to some club with her and her best friend Phoebe. Awww... music to my ears. I needed to dance it off with a straight rum and ice.

Cam called Mum to let her know she was taking me out and that I was fine (there were no mobile phones back then). I rerouted and headed off to my sister's for a night out. Little did I know that night would be life-changing in more ways than I could ever understand.

Ever.

THE FEELING

I love this
This feeling
It has my heart reeling
Wondering why...
There is no inappropriate touch
He would never think to put a hand on my crotch
Imagine, he loves me that much!
At first, his tenderness mystified my mind
His mannerisms always kind
Holds my hand while we walk

Looks into my eyes as we talk
Never will he disrespect me
We laughed, and I felt somewhat free
Years before faded and seemed somewhat insignificant
But sadly, I wonder...
If this is true love, is it meant for me?
Really...
Is this how love is meant to be,

Displayed in such a way like golden daffodils
And a sea of lilies in an untouched valley
No... this is not right
I question these new waves in hindsight
Surely, there is something wrong
This relationship is lasting far too long.
Dookie Dooks, you've grown used to the other kind
Sour filth that clothed your mind

Incense of sex and betrayal inhaled clouds your thoughts
This new experience has caused you to come off the familiar trail...
Flies down
Pinned down
Stay down
'Go down'
Turnaround
Pain so intense

You couldn't scream out
Dogs on heat, and you are caught in their fence
Spiritually, you put up a wall of defence
Dookie, girl, it's not been a kind world
Can you not accept that there is another side where true love resides?
Presented with bouquets of roses
Kissed gently on the lips

No tongue exposed
Buttons on your blouse stay closed
Really...
Oh, if I could have let you seen
That reliving ugliness was because of me
I couldn't let go of all we'd learnt
Life now was too lazy
Going out with friends

Holding hands

Naaa, that's crazy
Pretending we exchanged wedding bands
This kind of love suffocated your inner self...
The abused me
Cast out, hidden behind the vase of flowers on the shelf
No, thank you
I can't do this

I want intensity
Wake up the inner me
Am I dead?
No longer do I feel the slanderous touch
This kindness shown is too much
I need to break free
I've been inactive sexually
And I don't know how this could be

Is this love?
Is this love?
Is this love?
Is this love that I'm feelin'?
Like Bob, I wanna know now.
Although part of me was willing
I was just not able
Poor, soiled, tainted me

Blinded by the past,
I grab hold of my other half
No longer hidden on the shelf

The flowers have died
The vase put aside
No matter how I tried, I just couldn't hide.
Was this love?
When I grow old and look back

Hopefully, I will let you all know.

Part 3

**To Have
And To Hold**

Chapter 7

WHO'S THAT GUY?

I rummaged through Cam's wardrobe. She had amazing clothes, which, I might add, she made all herself as she was a seamstress. My hands rested on a wicked olive suit, a pencil mini skirt and front buttoned jacket on top. With my size-eight self, I rocked it with a pair of black stilettoes (which Cam had, and we were the same size). Make-up done, hair curled, and I was ready.

Phoebe, Cam and her husband Patrick also looked really good. I felt beautiful and looked beautiful. I'd made up my mind to forget about earlier that day. Cam was also irritated by Saul and encouraged me to forget him that night: 'Yuh too young to be so stressed over a man. Time to move on.'

Patrick drove us down to the Panama Night Club. The mere fact that we found a parking space pretty quickly was an indicator that the club was empty. Panama was known for having a slow start, but once it got going, it was a pretty decent club. I felt all eyes on us as we walked in, and I knew the men wondered which of us was with Patrick. The music was pumping, though, so we found a space near the wall facing the door to lime (A Trini word for hanging out) and have a good view of who was entering.

Every now and then, we nudged each other to have a giggle at a mismatched couple, an ugly brother or a badly dressed woman, passing the time as we did. The dance floor was getting full, and things were livening up, but we were still disappointed that not one single good-looking guy had come through the ticket area. It's not that Phoebe and I wanted a new man; it's more like we just wanted a good night of dancing with someone.

Cam wanted to go to the ladies'. We normally all went together, but we didn't want to lose our space. Patrick had already left to get our top-up of drinks, so Phebs and I stayed put. Standing and gazing around at the dead action with the lack of unattached men and undesirable single ones, we simultaneously froze. All we could do was excitedly pull at the sides of each other's clothes, have hot flushes and wear an uncontrollable grin as Prince Charming stepped into the club with a few other guys.

'Pheobeeeeeee! Oh, my gosh—looook at that fine godsend.'

Phoebe responded without a breath between her words, nearly tripping over her tongue. 'I know, I know, I knoooooow. Jeez, where's Cam? Trust her to miss this.'

He was of average height, Dougla (mixed Indian/South Asian and African descent, more or less), HANDSOME, dressed in a suit, looking sharp, with a smile to melt your heart and straight yet naturally curled hair

Saul? Saul who?

Cam appeared from the corner, and we pulled her in quickly. 'Look to your left slowly. DON'T look obvious, but clock that fine brotha. Oh, my gosh!'

Cam waited, then casually turned, and it didn't take a rocket scientist for her to know who we were drooling over. 'Who—him?' she asked casually without expression.

'Yesss,' I replied, still trying to dial this grin down to a smile.

Cam then spun completely around. At the same time, she said, 'Oh, him,' and walked towards him, leaving Phoebe and I dumbfounded on the spot, our mouths open, with 101 questions flooding our minds. 'She knows him. He's a friend of my sister's. How have I never seen this one? Phoebe, I thought you knew Cam's friends. How do you not know this guy?'

Phebs couldn't answer. She watched on in disbelief and shrugged her shoulders.

Trying not to look bait, Phebs and I kept peeking at them. Cam and that guy were having a conversation and sharing a laugh. After a while, they turned and started to walk over to us, no doubt for introductions.

It took everything within me to breathe with precision and look unphased by what stood before me. Cam had this grin on her face that I couldn't read as my mind was in a tizwas. How could anyone think in that situation?

'Kenrick, this is my friend, Phoebe,' he smiled, nodded and said hello, 'and this is my sister, Maria. Maria, meet Kenrick.' My smile broke into a grin I just couldn't keep it in. He looked me dead in the eyes as he said hello. My legs! Where were my damn legs? They felt like Jell-O O His smile made his eyes sparkle. He was breathtakingly handsome. Where had my sister met that guy? Why had I not seen him before? I knew her friends—well, most of them. Surely, I would have remembered him.

He was well-dressed in a fitted suit, a little goatee beard that matched his jet black, curly, Asian-type hair. His skin looked smooth without blemishes, and his smile was like a firearm as they shot bullets at me, and I felt weak.

He asked me to dance—like I was gonna say no! We danced and spoke about so many things that I didn't realise I had moved away from my party and him from his; it was just me and him.

He asked me if I wanted a drink, and I asked for a rum on the rocks. He brought me quite a few that night. I relaxed, and we spoke as if we had known each other for years. I learnt that he was going on holiday to Trinidad for the first time in a couple of months. I had already been, so I was telling him about all the places to go. I clean forgot about Cam, Patrick and Phoebe. Likewise, Kenrick never went back to the friends he came with.

The music played. We danced; we spoke—it was the perfect end to a rotten day.

The lights were turned on; the club was about to close. The last tune was being played, and it was time to say goodbye. It was then that I realised we'd spent all night together. Wow! And what a night it was.

Kenrick asked for my number, and I gave it to him without thinking twice. Cam, Patrick and Phoebe said their goodbyes. Cam said they'd be by the car that was just parked across the road. Kenrick walked me to the car, and we stood there for a moment. He said he would call me at 6 p.m. the next day. I smiled in agreement. He then leant over and gave me the softest, smoothest kiss on the cheek. He smiled as he saw me into the car before walking away.

Cam and Phoebe looked at me and cracked up laughing as I was in a daze.

He'd kissed me. I could still feel it on my cheek. No way was I washing off my make-up that night, as I wanted that feeling to stay.

I stared out the window on the way to Cam's. I asked her at least three times, 'Where did you meet him, and how long have you been friends?'

All Cam kept saying was, 'I'll tell you when we reach home,' so I gave up and stared out the window for the whole drive, a nerdy smile stuck on my face. I couldn't even hear their conversation.

As soon as we got inside and took off our coats, we badgered Cam to spill the beans: 'Where? When? Stop stalling.'

Cam turned around with a grin like the cat that swallowed the canary and said quite frankly, 'I don't!'

'You don't what? What's that supposed to mean? Cam, stop messing.'

'I mean just that,' she said, still smiling and trying to hold in a laugh. 'When I came out of the toilet, and you guys were going crazy about this guy, and you showed me who. On impulse, I turned and walked straight to him and said, 'Excuse me—my sister over there really likes you. I wonder if you would do me a favour and come over and meet her," and he did. The rest is history.'

Phoebe and I froze, our mouths open, catching flies.

'Cam, you didn't. You mean you never knew him? He's not a friend of yours?'

'Nope. You need a man. Get out of that relationship you have as all you do is argue. Time to move on.'

Gosh, so cutthroat.

The ground could've opened up and swallowed me in. 'Cam, I would've never spoken to him if I knew that was what you were going over to do. If I was a white girl, I would be beetroot red with embarrassment. What must he be thinking?' As I replayed the evening in my mind, I sunk deeper into my imaginary whirlwind hole. And to think I had asked him where he'd known my sister from. His reply had been that I should ask her when I got home! No wonder! What a plot! Cam was in stitches whilst Patrick and Phoebe chuckled and said how Cam had moved quickly to think of that plan and be so brave in a matter of minutes. Well, it was done, it had happened, it had worked. I got a kiss, and I had a phone call to receive at 6 p.m. the following day.

'Well, thanks a lot, sis. It sure paid off.' I laughed, but I still felt like an idiot. How embarrassing? OMG!

Time to sleep so tomorrow would come faster!

KISSING AWAY MY TEENAGE YEARS

Heated words
Same old issues throwing my feelings overboard
Complaints from my frustrated heart
Things that did not seem problematic at the start
His voice, my voice, I'm sure the universe is tired of hearing
Need to air out,
Get dressed and go out
Partnered with sister, brother-in-law and friend,
I intend to shack out
Standing dressed to impress
No longer feeling irritated and stressed
This is not the place to think of relationship mess
I look up, our eyes meet, all of a sudden, I can't feel my feet
Who is he?
Has he been sent to change me? Rearrange me? Complete me?
My life will never be the same
So starts my journey of unforgettable Joy, the exposed shame of past pain,
Seasons of sunshine, seasons of rain
Seasons where love abounds
And my womanhood is found
There is a tingling in the atmosphere
Goosebumps arise like chicken pox
My heart beats louder than a door knocks
Hello, Dookie Dooks
It's time

Alison Ryan -Chase

Real life is about to begin
You were charmed by his looks
Now, you are well and truly hooked
Two years, you were with Saul
You have to face him and start talking
Family ties
Little white lies
Your movements turn as you conjure up alibis
It's time
To kiss away teenage love
And embrace this sweet, handsome, Dougla man
He looks like the real kind of!
Only time will tell.
Is THIS love that I'm feeling?
Dookie, you gotta know now...

Chapter 8

WEAK IN ONE WEEK

The phone rang at 6.05 p.m. It was in the dining room, and Mum was in there doing some sewing. How on earth was I supposed to talk without baiting myself out? I didn't rush for the phone either like I was expecting a call either.

Mum was upset with me for staying out all night, leaving from Cam's to head to Saul's house to show my face for his mum's birthday (which I left prematurely as 6 p.m. was all that was on my mind). I made up an excuse that I had to go home early as Mum was fretting about my not helping her with Sunday dinner, which led to them (Berns and crew) asking why I went out and didn't tell them. Gosh, they made me feel so hot that I answered, falling over my tongue. 'Look, my sister decided at the last minute, and I didn't really think as I wasn't home.'

It was accepted without further questioning; phew! Saul was still a little sour with me, and to be fair, I was also, especially as I had Kenrick on my mind, and he weighed heavier on my scales.

'Hello?' I answered the phone and casually excused myself from the room, swiftly explaining that I couldn't hear properly. Mum gave me a cut-eye that would have cut me in two, but then I heard that familiar voice from the night before reply, 'Hello.' It was like I could see his smile through the phone, and it was carried in his voice. We spoke for a long while, and I had a fixed grin on my face the whole time, broken only by my mum's voice interrupting the call, telling me I'd been on it long enough as she was waiting on a call.

No, she wasn't. She just had sharp ears and must've realised it wasn't Saul I was talking to.

Kenrick and I made arrangements to meet up at the Panama nightclub the following week and promised each other we'd both be there.

I hung up the phone and took it back to the dining room. Mum was looking for a reason to have a go at me, but I moved fast. Before she could ask, I said it was an old school friend's brother I met up with out of the blue the night before. She blew hard through her nose like a bull looking to attack. If Mum was a Looney Tune, she'd have steam coming from her nostrils.

Did I care? Nope. My mind was full of Kenrick and our pending meeting. What was I going to tell my crew? How would I explain going to Panama for the second time in one week? How would I keep seeing Saul? What would I tell Bernel, Toni and Kacee? Good Lord!

As the week passed, I spent the time like a scriptwriter, trying to orchestrate a storyline that would explain how I knew Kenrick. He was definitely older, so he couldn't exactly be a school friend, so I kept with what I'd told my mum: he was a friend's brother. Bernel wasn't easily fooled and was a little suspect of the whole going to Panama's. I mean, it wasn't the greatest club, but I told her I was meeting one of my sister's good friends there.

'Really, Maria? Your sister?' It was so far-fetched it had to be true, right? I was already mixing up my story; I couldn't lie to save my life.

It sounded like Bernel had known for a while that things hadn't been right with Saul and me I'm sure she saw the old me creeping back. Saul was boring me.

No, that was not true; I really loved Saul.

Nope, that didn't fit either. I think Saul and I had slipped into a 'best friend zone'. I cared deeply for him, but at 18, did I really know what love felt like? We had started dating when I was 16, and I was in awe that I'd stayed in the relationship, judging by my track record. Saul looked out for me. He was caring, loving, sensitive, laughed at the same jokes and we enjoyed the same things... yep: best friends! I was fed up going out in a group, never on our own, the long walks to his home, the buses everywhere, and when we kissed, it was *always* the kiss on the cheek or a peck on the lips, that would define us as a couple, never an intimate, deep French kiss. All of the guys I'd seen before had cars. Yes, I was spoilt in some ways, but mostly, I was just used to hanging around with older people due to going out regularly with my older siblings, not too old, though, around the age of 20–28. Things were changing. I was changing. I was moving forward, but it seemed like a vertigo where I was being pulled forward and my friends seemed to be way behind me, with Saul farther back still.

Saturday arrived, and I was excited and anxious. It was proving impossible to shake off my friends, and I was spiralling in a well of lies to cover the fact that I'd met a guy who, in just one week, had stolen my heart.

Panama's was rocking. There was a nice crowd. I kept scanning the room, every now and then, turning to look at the door behind me. Berns was watching me, and it seemed as if I was annoying her. She and I were great friends but so were she and Saul. She'd known him longer and didn't want to see him get hurt. Like I said before, he was like a brother to her.

Berns and I had spoken about the cracks in my relationship with Saul, and she said she would be there for me if I stayed with him or if we broke up. What she didn't want was for me to two-time him.

Through the side of my eye, I saw Kenrick walk in, and the smile I'd practiced hiding burst through like the sun from clouds. I went towards him, forgetting whom I was with, willing my legs to keep me up as he had me spellbound.

Ken kissed me hello with a smile that irradiated his face. We spoke briefly, and I brought him over to introduce him to the girls. As I imagined, they were all mesmerised, and Berns smiled like she understood why I had been the way I was lately.

The atmosphere shifted, and we continued to enjoy the evening. I noticed that Bernel was a little edgy and often looked towards the door, but I just assumed she was amusing herself as we normally did, looking at which guys were walking in, and what other women were wearing.

There was a gentle tap on my shoulder, and I turned around to see Saul standing behind me with a sort of smile that I wasn't sure was a smirk, saying, 'Caught you.'

I smiled in surprise.

'Hey, what are you doing here?,' I said. 'Thought you said you weren't coming.'

'Well, I changed my mind.'

Saul smiled as I looked at Kenrick, but I held it together and introduced them. Luckily, I'd spoken to Kenrick about Saul. He knew he was my current boyfriend, and I was about to break up with him, so he wasn't entirely surprised. I realised that Bernel knew he was coming and that they'd planned to do this as they were trying to sus out my off movements as of late. Nevertheless, I felt betrayed to know they would scheme like that.

The rest of the night, I played yoyo! I wanted to be with Kenrick, but I obviously had to stand with the guys and Saul. Luckily, Kenrick realised my predicament; we had already spoken a couple of times in the week about my relationship with Saul and what my friends were like. He kindly said goodbye and that it was nice catching up with me loud enough for them to hear. He turned to the others and said his goodbyes. and that it was nice to meet them, and he left.

I refused to look flustered. The sheer annoyance at being set up by my friends kept my temper simmering but steady the whole way through. They couldn't read my body language; I was like an unpublished cipher!

The rest of the night was a bit dull as I had nothing much to say to any of them, to be honest, and I was upset with Saul, not from that night but just in general. We left soon after Kenrick, sharing cabs as usual. Also, as usual, I was the last drop off. As I rode home, looking out the window at the droplets of rain and the dazzling images of the streetlights, I wondered where things were going. Someone was going to be hurt, either me for living the life I was stuck in because of my extended family and friends not really getting what I wanted, or Saul and our friends if I broke up with him. Arrrrrrgggggh! It was too much! I needed to sleep. Hopefully, everything would be made clear in the morning. All I knew at that moment in time was that I was bewitched and under Kenrick's spell, his smile, his touch, his eyes, his voice. I wanted to see more of him, and I did in the weeks that followed.

Kenrick came regularly to see me. We went for long drives, pulled over in country lanes and kissed passionately. I mean, *really* kissed! Not just the pecks on the lips I'd had for the past two years; I mean intimate tongue kisses that repeated three words over and over again with each touch: I want you.

It wasn't long before we actually went all the way. I felt tense like a virgin but he was gentle with me and took the lead. His flesh was soft and warm, his hands gentle and soft. My mind raced. 'Oh, my gosh, Ken. This was it. Kissing was one thing, but I overstepped the mark when I allowed Ken to penetrate me sexually. Saul and I weren't married, but I felt as if I'd committed adultery!

I didn't know how to tell Saul I wanted to end our relationship. I was definitely living a lie now, definitely cheating on him and distancing myself from him and my friends as my face couldn't lie. When they spoke to me, I felt hot, and the heat rose to my cheeks.

Kenrick and I made wild, passionate love every chance we got. As soon as we saw each other, it was like he undressed me with his eyes, and I became weak, as my legs always turned to jelly when I saw him. Realising how intense we were, we decided I should go on the pill as we took risks every time. I soon became desensitised to Saul and what my friends thought.

I longed to be touched that way. It was different from the sordid hands that used to grope me and make me ashamed and disgusted way back in the past. Maybe I was grown and being 18 made a difference to my mindset. I also met some of Ken's close friends, who met up every Friday night (lads only), but I became Ken's right arm, so to speak, so I seemed to have broken the mould of not bringing girls with on Friday night when he started taking me along. They didn't seem to mind as their night consisted of games of dominoes and blackjack, which gave me a chance to show my skills and laugh about the competition of the game, and I fitted in just fine.

It was a couple of months into the relationship when Ken headed off to Trinidad for the first time. It was the longest three weeks without him, but I used the time to see more of my friends. I hadn't spoken of Ken much after that night in Panama's. I needed that dust to well and truly settle. I became satisfied with my double life, and Mum started to get used to Ken as he started to come around more. The thing that made her change was that I had a minor knee operation that had me bed-bound for a few weeks, and I became depressed. Mum didn't see Saul set foot in the house even once to come and see me, but Ken came every day. He drove over 20 miles to see me every night. One night, he lifted me out of the bed and carried me downstairs into his car to take me for a drive. Oh, yes, Mum loved all of that, and she started to like Ken very much.

They say that absence makes the heart grow fonder. My gosh, wasn't that the truth? Whilst he was away, we spoke on the phone daily every time he had the chance. I just knew I would end up being solely with him, but when would I pick up the nerve to tell Saul and explain to the guys why we'd broken up? I didn't want to be seen as a two-timer (although I was, big time). I needed a reason like we'd drifted apart or we were more like friends.

It was the longest three weeks. Ken came back, and as my home was en route to his from the airport, he stopped by before heading home. Oh, my—smile; his smile. It was obvious how much we missed each other. He didn't stay very long as he'd flown all night and hardly slept, but he and I both knew we couldn't last another moment, and it was highly unlikely, had he gone home, that he wouldn't have made it back down to mine due to jet lag. It didn't matter now. I'd seen him, and that was all I needed.

I was heading into a tornado; the more I delayed speaking to Saul about breaking up, the harder it got. Kenrick was okay and understood in the early part of our relationship, but things had become more serious, and he was starting to get a little edgy about the whole thing and couldn't understand why I was delaying. He said it felt like I was seeing both of them at the same time. Was I? I know I wasn't, but then, truth be known, I was.

I rang Saul and told him I wanted to meet and asked if he could come over. I was fed up with taking the bus to his and walking so long to his house. I had to make sure and tell him to come on his own as it was standard that one or two of the gang would tag along. Why, I never knew, but it irritated me and made me feel resentful about the whole relationship. I was just tired.

Saul and I met near my house as, again, I was fed up with taking the bus to his and walking so long to his house. It wasn't normal for me to ask him over, so he knew something was up. I didn't want to stay home, so we took a walk outside. There was a long silence before I came out with the fact that we needed to break up as we obviously weren't how we used to be, and it was frustrating, and I didn't feel like we had the same love for each other anymore.

Saul didn't agree. He liked our relationship and thought we could make it work. He apologised for not showing me the attention he should have as a boyfriend and said that he would change. He even suggested that we get engaged after Christmas.

None of it could have changed my mind. Who plans an engagement? It's supposed to be a surprise to the girl, right? I knew I would've softened and agreed to it all, but there was one thing that stood in the way: Kenrick. I wanted him. He made me feel like a woman, he drove, he was older, he was more mature, he took me out, and we were sexually attracted to each other. Saul just didn't weigh up.

He asked about Kenrick, if I was seeing him, and if that was what this was all about. I didn't dare admit it and say yes. I couldn't let them know I'd been seeing Ken all that time, never mind that it so wasn't like me to two-time. It wasn't my fault. I hadn't planned it. It just happened. I fell into a whirlwind and was trapped in the spin.

No matter what Saul suggested, I had no choice but to stick to my guns: no! He kept on about Kenrick, and I said, time and again, that yes, he liked me, but we were just friends.

'How could you be friends with a big man like him? What could be his interest in you but to take advantage? Why, Maria? How old is he?'

I stuttered. He was asking too many questions, and I didn't like being cornered. 'He's not that much older, Saul, he's…' How old was he? I had no idea; I hadn't thought to ask! I made up an age. 'He's 23, and I don't see why we have to keep talking about him.'

'Look, Saul, we've changed. It's not like that. I'm just fed up, and I don't want this anymore. Can't we just be friends? I mean, that's how we behave already. Nothing will be different, will it? Be honest.'

There was silence. Saul hung his head. I felt a wave of sadness, but at the same time, I felt relief it was finally done. I had told him.

I walked him to the bus stop and waited for the bus to arrive. I said I was sorry and that we would still be good friends, as I didn't see why that should change.

He got on the bus, and I turned and walked home. A burden had been semi-lifted; all I had to do was tell Bernel and the rest of them.

Saul and I had been an item for two years. Seeing us together was the norm. It was also expected, so going out with him now seemed weird. Like, where did we stand when in a group? Did I laugh at his jokes? Did we complement each other when we were dressed to go out like we used to? It was harder than I thought at first, but we got better at it.

Kenrick and I blossomed. I still kept our relationship on the down low as I didn't want my friends to think I'd broken up with Saul to go out with Kenrick, which I had; I was in denial.

I told Bernel that same evening as I wanted her to hear it from me first. Surprisingly, she was quite sympathetic and understood. All she wanted was for me to break it off with Saul if I knew my heart wasn't his. Berns was no fool, and I said no more to pretend I thought she was.

Kenrick and I grew inseparable. He came around and chilled with me at home nearly every evening. Sometimes, we stayed home and sometimes, we went out, just me and him, with no friends tagging along.

My friends got to know about Kenrick—I couldn't hide it anymore. Saul's brother wasn't impressed. Neither were his parents, but they got over it after a while. Our group still met up from time to time. It was a little awkward, but we all were just too great friends for my actions to infringe on that. Bernel, Toni and Kacee got to know Ken and grew to like him very much.

I felt like I'd grown. I asked Ken about his age: he was 28. Twenty eight, and I was just 18 and gobsmacked! I had no idea he was *that* old, a whole 10 years! Did I care? No. We were too far gone in our relationship, and I loved him, his maturity, his smile, his ways. The way he handled me made me feel clean when he touched me. It wasn't dirty. That was it, wasn't it? Love? It wasn't nasty. I consented. I said yes, and he touched me intimately because I'd allowed it and not because he was a greedy old man wanting a grope.

Months passed, and we started talking about the future, conversations about children and marriage. I'd always wanted it the right way: marriage first and then babies. I didn't want to be like some school friends I'd met over the years who'd had babies and were single mothers because their boyfriends had bailed, and I didn't want to be like my sister, Cam, who was forced to be married due to her being pregnant.

My heart and passion grew with a force, and Ken and I made the decision for me to come off the pill.

And I did.

METAMORPHOSIS OF LOVE

Confusion
My mind runs to and fro
Can't step forward, yet I refuse to step back
Passion runs high, but I'm too stuck to let go
I can't seem to get my heart and mind to comply
I've reached an unnatural high
How do I tell a fading love goodbye?
Living a lie yet living a truth
Sitting back and waiting, my whole body inhales, then sighs
Intimacy has birthed a soul tie
Attempts to cover up hurdles into more lies
Dookie Dooks has a new outlook
No longer the stench of impurity
But an intense sexuality
Could this be due to maturity?
His hands, his kiss, his lust
Stripping away years of indecent touch
My body screams out in delightful pain
Fills me again and again
These wanton thoughts drive me insane
I've got to speak out and get rid of this hidden shame
I've got to tell Saul I don't feel the same
Without revealing my lover's name
His hands, his kiss, his lust
Our lust, our kisses, our hands
We nestle and entwine in invisible wedding bands
What was it that Jesus wrote with the stick in the sand?

Breathe...
I am not a married woman caught in adultery
But a young woman crying out for love
Not the descriptive love of my youth
That interpreted an ugly false truth
Now a need manifests in me
A desire to cultivate my lover's seed
My heart pulsates
My mind is overruled
Passion is about to map out my fate
Pray this new love does not have me fooled
This is me...
A new feeling has arisen
Dookie Dooks, you are entering a new season
Life as you know it is about to be rearranged
Get ready for the change.

Chapter 9

BROTH VS MANGOES!

Weeks flowed into months, and my cloud cuckoo land feeling did not fade. It was the most serious I'd been with anyone. I mean, I thought Saul and I were a solid couple, but this was way different. Meeting Ken's family was not as daunting as I thought. I thought our age difference would be an issue with them, but they all received me with warmth. It was at the christening of his sister's son that I first met most of his family. He had a sister, three brothers and a number of nieces and nephews. Oh, and another thing: Kenrick had a son.

Well, I shouldn't be surprised, really, seeing as Kenrick was ten years older than me. Ironically, his son was eight years old, ten years younger than me. I looked at him, thought of the age gap between Ken and me and closed my eyes to extinguish my thoughts. It was crazy imagining him as my boyfriend. It was outrageous, yet it seemed fine.

It was July, and I was preparing to go to my cousin's wedding in Trinidad with my mum. I was to be a bridesmaid, so I was very excited. I had been in a relationship with Ken for just over five months, but it felt as if we'd known each other for years. Again, being separated from him would prove to be very difficult. I know it is said that absence makes the heart grow fonder, but how much fonder of each other could we be? We were surely at our peak! I was only going for three weeks and hoped it would fly by.

Ken came to see us off, and we promised to stay in touch (yes, I know, it was only going to be three weeks!). Though I love flying, the flight was not enjoyable at all. The food seemed off, and the turbulence left a lot to be desired. I was certainly glad when we arrived safely. It was good to feel the humidity and smell the tropical

fragrance in the air.

My uncle, who lived in town (Port of Spain, the capital), picked us up. We were to stay by him for a few days, acclimatise, then head down south. I asked to use the phone as soon as I got there to call Ken and let him know that we had got there okay. As usual, my legs turned to jelly, and my heart was full when he answered the phone. It was a very quick call as it was an overseas call and expensive; the next day, I brought a bunch of international phone cards.

The first few days was spent getting over my jetlag, seeing more friends and family, and catching up with cousins and aunties and uncles, marvelling at how much I had grown. It was mango season, and the whole country seemed to smell of them. Before long, my gut was full, and I couldn't stomach sucking on one more, let alone smelling them.

After a few days, we ventured down south, and it was a beautiful sight, driving through the winding country roads full of tropical plants and palm trees, though you couldn't get away from the sight of badly mutilated dogs lying in the roads from being knocked down. I wondered who had the awful job of clearing them up, as when you passed the same place a day later, they were gone!

As we approached the house, I saw my cousins and auntie waiting to greet us. There was excitement in the air. Mum let out a giggle, and I had the biggest grin. We loved our family to the max, and they were very fond of us, too. There was a jovial few minutes of greetings and laughter. All talk was on the approaching wedding, and my cousin, Nikay, beckoned for me to come into the back bedroom to show me our bridesmaid dresses. I needed to try mine on as soon as possible in case any alterations needed to be made. To be honest, the dress wasn't the greatest of designs, and Nik and I weren't too keen on it at all. The only saving grace was that there were another five of us who would be in the same dress on the day! We could cope with that.

Nik and I went everywhere together. She took me to all her hangouts, and when we were at home, we helped with preparations for the wedding. Our family was huge, and there was no need to waste money on outside caterers or wedding planners. We were all quite capable, and from the youngest to the oldest, there was something you could put your hands to.

Before the wedding, we (my cousins and I) decided to have a girls' night out. It was nice being with them as we were all about the same age, though they were a year or two—or three—older than me, so Mum didn't fuss over my safety.

The evening began with us liming in a couple of bars before heading to where the Soca fete was. By that time, I'd had a couple of straight rums and was feeling nice.

As we entered, the music was jamming, and people were getting on real bad. The atmosphere was on fire. We ordered drink rounds, and once again, I requested my signature rum on the rocks. My cousin always ordered me doubles as she thought the drinks looked small. It was the norm for 'ladies' to drink their drinks through straws, even with beer bottles, but not me. I took my drink like a man; no straws needed.

The party was pumping, but I started to feel a little off. I normally smoked, especially when drinking, but the Benson & Hedges brand of cigarettes wasn't the same as in England. They were much stronger and I didn't like them at all. I guess being in Trinidad would help me give them up. After a couple of hours, I was on water as I felt so queasy. I was so happy when we all decided it was time to hit the road and head home.

My cousins were real kicksin[1] and had a good laugh at my expense as they thought I was a little wasted. It just wasn't like me. How much had I really drunk? Maybe it was because I couldn't enjoy a fag with it, or maybe it was the humidity. Whatever it was, I felt like crap. Everything spun. I spun. I closed my eyes, and the spinning was as intense as a rollercoaster. Thankfully, I didn't feel like I had to vomit. I think my body and mind knew I had a phobia when it came to vomiting, so I switched off that thought (it wasn't permitted!), but the nausea was horrendous. I managed to fall asleep but sitting upright as I feared being sick.

In the morning—well, mid-morning—I awoke, and I felt as if my insides had churned over and like my body wasn't my own. Who punched me? Who had I fought? What had I eaten? Was it food poisoning? The feeling was BAD. My cousins giggled, but they were concerned about how rough I looked.

'Maria, girl, wha' happen to you, girl? Yuh cyant tek de rum? Yuh gone soft or what?' Their giggling burst into laughter. I laughed, too, but my gosh, it hurt. I was truly wasted and couldn't function.

Now, there was a trick to getting over a hangover. It was to have a drink of what got you drunk. But I wasn't

---

[1] Trini word for 'play around'

drunk! I was in my right senses. I just started to feel really, really bad. There was no way I could have stomached a straight rum at that moment, so cure number two: fish broth!

My older cousin Glenroy took pity on me and said, 'Hold tight, baby girl. Ah go fix yuh up ah nice li'l broth. You'll feel better in no time.' Knowing a cure was coming, that the feeling had an end, was the best feeling. I told myself there was no way I was having a drop more rum whilst on that holiday.

I could just about move to shower and let the water barrel's cool water fall on me. As I came out, the aroma of the broth filled the wood-panelled house. Nik chilled with me and waited for me to function again. Gladly, I wasn't feeling as badly as the night before.

Glenroy finally bought me a small bowl of broth. The medicine was the broth itself, no provision, dumplings or fish, just the water. I sipped it slowly, thankful that with every spoonful, I actually felt soothed.

I got my energy back within an hour. Talk about happy! That sickness was nothing I'd ever felt before, but now it was all over. Nik had some pineapple and mango cut up in a bowl and came back into the bedroom to sit with me, but I had to beg her to take the fruit out. The smell was unbearable!

She left momentarily, then came back into the room, looking rather thoughtful, like Sherlock Holmes's sidekick Watson. Nik looked at me as she approached the bed, her eyes not leaving me.

'What?' I said.

'Maria, maybe this has something to do with your periods.'

I looked up. 'My periods? No, I never get sick like this with my period, just slight cramps.'

Nik frowned. 'That's not really what I meant. I mean like, when was your last period?'

Now, it was my turn to frown. 'I don't know. I'm never regular. In fact, it's very erratic.' I felt my facial expression go a little blank as I began to see where Nik was going with this.

'Nik—' My eyes were fixed in a stare as my mind worked overtime.

'Think about it, Maria. You real have a problem with mangos and smoking. I've never known you to get high on rum or ever seen you with a hangover and to top it off, you can't even remember the last time you had your period!'

'Could it be? Oh, my gosh—a baby?

'Naaa… No way. And besides, we only just decided for me to come off the pill recently. How quick do these things really take?' I was flabbergasted. So many thoughts crossed my mind.

A smile grew. There was actually the possibility I was carrying Ken's baby. Oh, my gosh! My smile grew even more. Then, as fast as it grew, it vanished.

My mum! How on earth—what on earth—would I tell her? What would she do? The feeling of dread was written all over my face.

Nik looked at me, put her arm around me and with comforting words, told me not to worry about it as we were only speculating. The best thing to do was enjoy the rest of my holiday and just watch myself to see if there was a pattern of weird things happening to me. It was easier said than done!

A few days passed, and even though there was pure excitement in the air, I couldn't help but help but think about the conversation Nik and I had. Should I tell Ken? What was the point? Tell him what? I wasn't sure. No test had been done — why worry, right?

I noticed that my mum was watching my movements a lot. She was not stupid. Without asking me questions, she was looking at me as in a huff all the time. I never said a word and played it like I was unaware. I had to suck it in, all the bad feelings, all the waves of nausea that seemed to creep up on me in the evenings, and I was so tired all the time. My excuse was that the sun was too hot, and it was just sunstroke or something. After all, there was the possibility that it could be my mind playing tricks on me, and it could really be that I was too hot in the sun.

The day of the wedding came. Everyone was running around, doing what had to be done. Nik and I had done our make-up and put on our bridesmaid dresses, with Nik moaning the whole time about how much she didn't like how the dress fit her. I was concerned that my dress wouldn't fit, but that was my paranoia, as even if I was pregnant, I wouldn't be showing yet.

The ceremony was long, and the heat was unbearable. It didn't help that every time I turned my head, there was my mother watching me. She suspected something was up, but it was like she didn't want to confront me and ask in case she heard what she didn't want to hear; hear what she already knew in her heart.

Heels are not for feet in that heat, and my feet were beyond hurting.

Straight after the ceremony, we went to take pictures, then on to the reception, and more pictures were taken. Whilst the speeches were going on, my rebellious cousin grabbed me and said, 'Let's get out of here, cuz. Our time and duty in these dresses are over,' so we snuck out to go home. The reception was just a five- to ten-minute walk away, so we got in, changed and chilled for a while as we were both tired. Our feet were painful and swollen from being in heels all day.

Then, we headed back to the reception, when the speeches had finished, and the music had started. The wedding was a huge success and beautifully done. The dancing continued into the night, and we all had a grand time, but, my gosh, I felt it the following day. I had a hangover, and I didn't even drink any alcohol!

It was getting ridiculous. There was really no doubt about it now; there were no other excuses, no tests were done, and only my observations of myself. Nik looked at me, and I at her, and we smiled knowingly: I was pregnant.

I was so glad I had Nikay, one of my best cousins, to confide in. That holiday was the closest we'd ever been. She teased me about Ken. She knew all about us and thought the love we shared was so cute. If it wasn't for her, I don't know how I would've coped over the last couple of weeks.

It was coming up time for us to leave and go back to England. I was sad to leave yet ecstatic to see Ken once again. He called again the night before we flew out, and I couldn't hold it. I told him of my suspected pregnancy and how Mum had been funny with me for days. He just said not to worry about it, just to enjoy my last few hours, and when I got back, I could sort out a test and deal with all the rest.

Packed and ready to head out, we said our goodbyes with kisses and hugs. No more would I have Nik to protect me from my mum's daggers and sarcastic comments. She actually packed some mangoes she was bringing back to England in the hold of the cabin above my seat on the plane; she definitely did that on purpose.

So, there I was, stuck on a night flight with the sickly smell of mangoes above my head. I had my normal evening nausea, so I just tried my best to sleep as there was nowhere to run and no seats to swap.

That was the longest flight, taking me on a journey of life I've never known before.

VINEYARD HARVEST

Like an aromatic vineyard
Grapes bulging with rich ripe juice
My body ignited cells to reproduce

Rewind...

A seed sown and planted
It waits...

Rewind...

Bodies embraced as hearts race
His touch is music
And I dance
I'm in a trance
Intoxicated by the essence of his love
He cups my breast
He hungers, I thirst
It is likened to an overdose of night nurse!
Ecstasy blows up, we burst
Then comes the rain
The drizzle of passion that drips soothingly off a leaf's tip
All is still
Exhale... now breathe,

Fast forward...

Tropical sun shows its face
Family and friends lovingly embrace
Out on the town, then home flat on my face!
What is this?
No to rum of the sweet Isle of T&T
It's the season for mangoes, but not for me
Intense nausea as the fruity smell fills my nose
I'm hot — I just need the open end of the water hose
Suspicions have arisen
Could it be there is a mini him, a mini-me
Encased in a cell on a wall
Clutching on so as not to fall
Waiting to be fed and manifest
Then, nine months later, await that first cry??
Stop. Breathe. It's okay

Press play...

Bae, I'm back from my holiday
Let's talk with words
That our bodies already spoke
Let this conversation confirm the revelation
Remember the vineyard?
The sweet fragrance of a full-bodied yield
My body ignited
The seed that was planted has reproduced
My lover, I am not afraid
I know you are with me to stay
No matter, come what may

Alison Ryan -Chase

We'll bring a healthy baby into this world
Regardless if a boy or girl
The rain fell
Now the sun is shining
Engulfing every cloud with a silver lining

Chapter 10

CLEAR BLUE

I slept for the majority of the flight. I couldn't understand why I felt really bad from 3 p.m. onwards and not only had nausea but it gradually increased until sleep fell on me. I thought morning sickness was called that because it happened in the morning! Thank goodness I was always tired, which made it easier to sleep through the long hours in the air with that pungent smell. I mean, was it just me or did the whole plane smell of ripe mangoes? The flight attendants served the usual rock-hard, cold muffins and finger sandwiches, which was a struggle to stomach at the best of times. I brightened up and put on my well-trained mask I wore around my mum. Whatever she was thinking (or dreamt!), I needed to throw her off until I was at least 100% sure. I did my best not to screw up my face about the smell as I saw her watching my every reaction, as if she had set up her own little test to justify her suspicions.

At the first convenient moment after we reached home, I went to get a pregnancy test at the chemist. My anxiety couldn't wait to go to the doctor. I went to the toilet and read the instructions over and over again reading each step again as I physically did the test. I thought I peed too heavily on it and would drown the test, but no, after the required waiting time that seemed like 30 minutes rather than three, there it was, the tell-tale cross of confirmation: positive.

There was no get-out clause, no going back. It was the nerves of telling my mother the news that was freaking me out. As for me, I was ecstatic. I was waiting for Mum to pop out to the shops in order to call Ken, but when the phone rang, it was him. Mum was still around and in earshot, so Ken did the talking as he knew by the way I was talking I wasn't alone. He asked, and I answered, 'Uh-hum, yes.'

There was a slight pause, and he told me everything would be all right and not to worry about a thing. He was going to come around later that evening. Just the thought of him coming over helped relax my nerves. I loved the way he was strong and mature. That is what I appreciated about our age difference. I felt safe.

There was a good reason I didn't want my mum finding out, why I was so scared. Well, there is a little detail I missed, and I guess once I tell it everything will make sense.

A few months back, Ken and I went out to a party and came back in the wee hours of the morning around five. Mum and Dad were awake as Dad was working a six to two shift. Mum was going to drop him to work so she could keep and use the car. I asked Mum if Ken could stay and sleep on the sofa as he was mega-tired, and he lived too far to drive safely. Mum was okay with it. Dad and I hardly spoke, but when Mum told him, he didn't mind either. Ken had built up a good relationship with my parents and trust with my mum. Since the time he'd taken me out when I had that mini-operation on my knee, she'd fallen in love with him and come to terms with the fact that I was no longer with Saul.

I went upstairs and brought down a sheet, blanket and pillows. Our sofa was a sofa bed, so Ken helped me pull it out flat. I made up the bed for him and went upstairs. My parents got ready to leave. Mum said she'd be back soon, and they left.

My mind went into fast gear. Ken and I were restricted as to where and when we got intimate as his parents were always home, and I had to be an inspector in my home, trying to work through my parents' shift schedule at work. My brothers and sister had all left home.

It would take Mum 20 minutes to drive Dad to work and 15 to 20 minutes back again. No one else was home. I'd had a few rums, and my head was sweet!

I went downstairs. Ken was already asleep. He'd had a few drinks, too, which added to his being too tired to drive. I gently lifted the blanket and positioned myself right next to him. I was already naked, and the alcohol had me aroused.

Ken awoke and stirred at the touch of my body. He was quickly aroused but came to his senses, saying it wasn't right as Mum had trusted him, yet he couldn't keep his hands off me; we couldn't keep our hands off each other.

Our body heat grew intense. As usual, images of the past came to my mind and I spent some energy brushing them aside. I had to keep my eyes open so the reality of where I was and with whom would stay. Making love with Ken was exactly that: making love. It wasn't the ugly stuff of the past; this was different. I didn't mind being touched by him. He made it okay, clean, even. There you had it: two bodies colliding in a mystical dance and exploding with a gush of ecstasy. Ken and I were both covered in beads of sweat. My body glistened with a shimmer of sweat that made me feel smooth all over. I breathed, smiled and cuddled myself in his arms.

'Maria, go back upstairs before your mum gets back,' he whispered.

I was in a cloud all by myself. Making love to Ken tingled all my senses, and I didn't want the feeling to end. 'I'll go in a minute,' I replied. I was tired of rushing. I just wanted to lie next to him for five more minutes. I was intoxicated not only by his love and his touch but also by the drinks I'd had earlier. I snuggled up into his arms and just lay there, drinking it all in and fell into a gentle, deep sleep.

It was that familiar rattle of keys that jolted me awake.

'MUM... SHIT! OH, MY GOSH!'

I shook Ken, but he was out like a light. I had come downstairs with no clothes on except my knickers, which were now hidden somewhere in the bed sheets. There was nowhere to run and definitely nowhere to hide. The dreaded footsteps came in the front door, and I swallowed hard as her figure came into the living room.

She gasped at the sight before her eyes, clothing me in a tremendous amount of shame. 'WHAT THE HELL AM I SEEING HERE? KENRICK? MARIA? NOOO NOOO, NOT IN MY HOUSE! TEK YOUR NASTY SELF UPSTAIRS. I TRUSTED YOU BOTH, AND LOOK WHAT I COME HOME TO.'

Well, her shouting awoke Ken, too, and as his senses kicked in, he soon realised what had happened, and he groaned, 'Oh, my God.'

I sheepishly grabbed a sheet to wrap myself with and ran past my mother with fear in my mind, kicking myself that I had not listened to Ken and gone to my bed when he'd said to.

There was no way he could go back to sleep now as Mum quarrelled loudly with herself about the disrespect and mistrust. I heard Ken get dressed and go into the kitchen to speak to Mum. He had a calming voice, and as he began to speak, Mum grew quieter. As he was speaking. I came downstairs, fully dressed He apologised profusely and agreed that what we had done was a great disrespect and abuse of her trust. He said that if he was in his right mind, he never would have taken advantage of the moment, but the alcohol had clouded our judgement. Mum turned and looked at me. I swore that it was the first time, and it must've been because I was a little tipsy from the alcohol, and I don't know what came over me.

Mum actually brought it! She was still mad, but not enough to kill me mad. This sobered the both of us up. I mean, how EMBARASSING was that?

Ken left after apologising to Mum again, and he said he would see me later; I dared not kiss him goodbye. As soon as he left, I went straight to my room. Sleep was far from me now. All I could do was replay that morning's event in my mind, and I shuddered with each recollection.

Ken came back later that evening, as promised. He was so mature—he'd done wrong and humbly apologised. Not even my mum could resist his smile, and I thought more of him as most guys my age would've run and never looked back. Ken also chastised me for not listening to him. I accepted that I was wrong, and we put it behind us. Well, Ken and I did. Mum made it a point to keep her eyes on us from then on out.

So this is why my mother's eyes became daggers in Trinidad! Since that traumatic episode, I think she suspected I would eventually come home pregnant, and three months later, I did! Although she suspected I was pregnant in Trinidad, I guess she didn't want to upset her holiday by bringing it up, but her actions spoke volumes.

How was I to tell her now that I was carrying Ken's baby?

Days passed, and Ken and I were excited with our secret. I went to the doctor, and he did a urine test to confirm I was pregnant and almost eight weeks' gestation.

I came up with a plan. The old people say, 'Yuh catch fool to play wise'—I needed a way to tell my parents, and I had a plan: Cam!

My sister was awesome, but she was terrible at keeping secrets. I called her up on the phone. 'Hi, sis—how are you?' I began. 'Hey, I got a secret, but you can't tell ANYONE. Not yet, anyway. Ken and I are expecting a baby.'

She let out a scream of delight, full of excitement. Cam congratulated me and asked who knew and how far gone I was. I told her our cousin Nik knew, and that was it. She asked if Mum knew, but I told her no, not yet, that it was a bit difficult. Cam understood that as Mum had given her a hard time when she was pregnant with her daughter, although that had been 10 years before. Still, it hadn't changed how Mum saw sex and pregnancy out of wedlock.

Cam was genuinely happy for us and made sure that I remembered it was she who had introduced us... how could I forget?

I left it for a couple of days and waited for my mum's countenance to change, which would be my signal that Cam had let the cat out of the bag. The plan was that if

I told Cam, and she told Mum, it would soften the blow when I told her, as she'd already know, and it worked.

Mum was in the kitchen, so I waited for her to be nearly finished as the smell of cooking in the evening had me really queasy. Things had been a little tense between Mum and I, but she was calm. I figured it was best if I just got it over with—what could she do? Kill me? The beauty of it all was that I knew Cam had already told her.

'Mum, I know you won't like this very much, but I am pregnant, and Ken and I are happy and intend to keep it. I know you may be disappointed, but I do believe we will cope just fine.'

The silence was deafening! She turned and looked at me and said she done knew already (said she'd dreamt it!), and that I couldn't hide very well, always sleeping and not eating properly.

'Well, I hope you don't think you can stay here, cuz I don't want no big belly chile in my house, so yuh better look for somewhere to go,' she said. With that, she walked off. I guess that wasn't bad, but it wasn't good either.

My dad came to me later that evening to say Mum told him and to never mind her; she'll come around eventually. She had been the same with my sister at first and softened after. Now look: 10 years later, and they have a great relationship. It was true. I just had to ride it out.

After that, I was free to tell everyone. My brothers were happy, as well, and my cousin, Shantel, who I hardly saw anymore but was still very close to, was excited for us, too.

I met up with the girls, Bernel, Toni and Kacee. Telling them was the hardest, as for them, Ken and I had been together just a few months, considering that about a month was secret in the beginning whilst trying to break up with Saul without a mess.

They were shocked and a bit worried for me. 'What about your life, Maria? Holidays, travelling the world, your career. You can't do that with a baby.' They were concerned and, I guess, rightly so. They were just getting used to Kenrick, and they were—we were—young and had our lives in front of us, young and free.

I reassured them that I would be okay and that Ken was right by my side. In turn, they smiled and gave me hugs, and we ended the night in good humour, bussin' jokes as we always did. As for Saul, Patrick and their parents, I let the girls break the ice on that one as I did with Cam and Mum. I was so close to Saul's family that I felt I had let them down, but when I saw them at a function a few weeks later, they were just as kind and loving to me. There were no hard feelings, but just like the girls, they were a little concerned that I had been trapped by this older guy who seemed to come from out of nowhere. I also reassured them that I was very happy, and Ken was a gem. He looked after me and treated me so well. I felt so special with him. He was my world. Saul was hurt, I know, but he was dating again, which I hoped had cushioned the blow of my situation.

Days turned to weeks and weeks to months, and Mum still grunted good mornings and didn't pay much attention to me. My aunts and uncles were very happy for me and Ken. They liked us as a couple, and Ken was always respectful and social with them. Mum was just being stubborn and set in her ways.

After my aunt Belinda had a word with her, she came around. I was into my sixth month by then, and my stomach was really showing. Mum came home one day from work. She had made a maternity, front-fastening nightshirt with a matching romper suit for the baby. It was unisex, and it was beautiful. I was so happy and grateful for a sign that she was talking to me again.

At the time of my pregnancy, I already had six nieces—my half-sister and Cam each had a daughter, my eldest brother Teddy had two daughters, Curtis had one and my other brother Lincoln, who was the youngest of the boys, had one girl, too so it was inevitable that I would also have a girl. I didn't even consider it could be a boy. We chose a girl's name but not a boy's; that's how confident I was. Ken couldn't care less. He just wanted a healthy baby. Telling his parents wasn't so bad as they liked me, and I adored them, as well as his sister and brothers.

Three months to go, and a few big changes were about to take place. For one, the council found me a Mother and Baby Home. It was the start of moving out on my own. All of a sudden, I was going from a fancy-free teenager to a responsible adult. With Ken by my side and baby on the way, I was ready.

THERE'S A BLESSING IN THERE

There is a new unknown beat
A simple test has revealed
It was not my heart
But the one that grew from the seed sown
What is this disgrace?
That my mother would have me hide my face
Not letting me forget I was caught red-handed
Embraced in my sweetheart's arms
Captivated by his charm
Mother was remarkably candid
Not here in this home
If you are pregnant, then find your own.
My news was difficult to share
I wasn't sure of the response of the friends I held dear
But to my pleasant surprise
I came to realise
They loved me dearly and showed they cared
Does it really matter, though?
I have my lover and best friend by my side
He says he'll always be there for me
With him, I shall grow and be free
We've created ourselves a new destiny
For who knows if this was meant to be?
I do
No longer touched indecently
But I need to remove those sins from my memory
Tell me

Tell me they will go away
When I close my eyes
And next to Ken I lie
Let my inner me see
A break in soul ties
Illegal touches and deafen my ears to past lies

Chapter 11

FIRST

I went to view the Mother and Baby Home, although I couldn't see the point as I had no choice but to move in there. It wasn't ideal, but it was temporary. Apparently, it was just a pit stop for women needing emergency accommodation, and I guess Mum wanting no 'big belly woman' in her house meant I was classified as an emergency. I was told the policy was that it was not permitted for a mother to stay there once her baby had reached three months old, so that was encouraging. Soon, I'd have my own place. I'd officially be a grown-up!

A lovely lady opened the door of the large, three-storey house. Once inside, I saw it was a multiple-occupancy home. The lady was middle-aged and Caucasian and greeted me warmly, introducing herself as the landlord who lived on the top floor of the building.

She took me down to the basement, where there was a double room that had a stove, a single wardrobe, a fridge, a table, chairs and a bed. It was clean and tidy. The bathroom and toilet were in the hallway and were to be shared with another girl, who had the room next to mine. Everything was clean and tidy. There weren't many house rules, but two stood out: all male visitors had to leave by 10 p.m., and boyfriends were not allowed to sleep over. Great!

I was handed the keys. All that was left was to move in.

I didn't have a lot of items. I mean, I was only moving from Mum's, and the only belongings I had were my clothes. I couldn't bring that much with me anyhow, as most of my clothes didn't fit for obvious reasons, and the room didn't have much storage space other than a small wardrobe, kitchen cupboard and draw unit.

I loved it. There were only two rooms in the basement, mine and a girl called Mary had the other. There was also a side basement door we could use to come in and go out. Mary and I became quick friends and made a pact to watch each other's backs regarding men, as the no men after 10 p.m. and the no sleeping over rules didn't wash too well with us or our partners. To wait so long to finally have my own space without sneaking around parents or finding a 'lovers' lane' to have my own pad, even though it was temporary, and Ken still was not allowed to stay over? No way.

You'd think I would be glad to stay on my own, but it became lonely as I was in my seventh month, on maternity leave from work and restless. Ken was at work all day but I found joy in listening out for his distinctive car engine, timing when the engine stopped to him reaching the door. I enjoyed the change. In my mind, I felt like we were a couple living together, which we were, in a way, as Ken hardly ever stayed home at his parents' any more. It was nice not having to sneak around to be together in an intimate way. We were free, yet I missed my friends. I missed the part of me that was still a teenager.

Bernel had taken up a new catering manager course, Toni was working full-time in the city, and Kacee had gone away travelling on a working holiday, so I was pretty much friendless during the day. I spent my days shopping for groceries. We couldn't do a big shop as the fridge was small, single and fit for one person. There was a day that I spent watching TV—the baby had me like a sluggard the closer I got to my due date. The hours went by with me watching the omnibus of *Neighbours* and *Home and Away*. I heard Ken's car and timed it, as I usually did, for him to reach the door and open it. Moments later, he walked in to see me with the carpet sweeper in one hand and the other hand on my back.

'Here, baby, leave that to me and go rest.' I smiled, said thank you and sat down. I didn't feel bad as I had washed the dishes earlier, and I had to carry this baby 24/7.

A few days later, there was a knock on my door. It was Mary and the landlady. Mary was trying her hardest to hold back a grin.

The landlady explained that the council had found me temporary accommodation. It was apparently a large house divided into two flats, which was offered to Mary first as she had been at the home before me. Mary requested that I take the other flat as we got on, and the landlady agreed. There was no viewing as it was that or nothing. Once you were offered a place, that was it. If you turned it down, the council would not offer another, and you were on your own.

Moving was easy. As it was a small room, it only took a couple of car rides. After moving, we decided it would be best to spend a couple of weeks at my mum's as I approached my thirty-ninth week and the baby could've come at any time, and my parents' home was much closer to the hospital.

I hardly saw Berns and the girls. One night, they were going out to a local club where our mutual friend was a DJ. I was not only 40 weeks pregnant, but it was also my due date. I insisted on going out too, Bernel thought I was crazy, but she knew she couldn't stop me. I was so bored and fed up I needed an outlet. I also hoped that dancing would cause the labour to start!

The music was pumping when we got there. It was so good seeing Jimmy on the deck, spinning tunes. He was happy to see me and surprised to see me pregnant. When he asked when I was due, his eyes nearly popped out of his head with my answer.

I danced until I ran out of steam. Did it cause my labour to start? No. Did it cause an excruciating backache?

Most definitely, yes, and swollen feet, but it was worth it. I had a great time.

A week later, as we were waiting for the first tinge of pain and my appointment date to be induced, Mum, Ken and I decided to have a video night. I needed some fresh air, so I opted to go to the video rental shop. Heaven knows why I chose *The Adventures of Babysitting* and *Three Men and a Baby*. Obviously, I had babies on my mind!

We finished watching one, and I told Ken to wait until I got back from the toilet to put the other one on. I'm not sure if I was bursting or the baby was resting on my bladder, but I was getting these weird sensations every so often, and I couldn't concentrate on the movies.

Typically, there was a trickle of pee, which meant the baby was resting on my bladder. As I wiped myself, the tissue had a pink pastel colour to it. I wasn't sure if my eyes were playing tricks on me, so I wiped again, and there it was: a streak of mucus with slight blood in it. I grinned, but there was an undertone of fear. This was surely it. What a doddle! If this was labour, it was a walk in the park!

There. Again, I felt that sensation ring across my back. I'd never been pregnant before, so what did I know? 'd assumed that as the baby grew in the stomach area, that's where the pain would be.

Not wanting to panic Mum and Ken over a false alarm, I called down to say I wouldn't be long and got ready to time the next sensation.

Seven minutes. Okay, cool.

I went downstairs, and Ken started the movie. Seven minutes later, there was another sensation, but this one was a tiny bit more prominent than the one before. I got a little panicked and blurted out, 'I think I'm in labour!'

They looked at me, startled. I told them all that had happened upstairs and reassured them both that I was fine. Mum suggested I go have a warm bath and call the hospital to let them know what was going on.

As I ran the bath, I called the labour ward. My voice was calm yet a little excited. I explained in detail, and they were quite happy for me to stay home as things were moving slowly along.

Ken paced up and down. I grabbed his arm gently and kissed him on his cheek, letting him know I was okay. He smiled. 'This is it, girl.'

Mum and Ken left me alone to bathe. Mum fussed around, making sure my bag was packed. Her excitement made me giggle.

I stood up to get out of the bath, took hold of the towel and took a step out the bath when a pain struck me so powerfully from out of nowhere that I couldn't move except to scream out.

Mum came running up the stairs and barged into the bathroom. She helped me out of the bath and looked at the time: five minutes since the last contraction.

I dried myself and was hit again with a piercing pain that crippled me. I opened my mouth, but not a sound came out. I was breathless.

Four minutes since the last contraction.

Ken rang back to the labour ward to tell them I wasn't coping. They couldn't quite believe it, considering they had spoken to me just 30 or so minutes beforehand.

Ken passed the phone to me, and I spoke through gritted teeth. The transformation had been astonishing. Again, the pain shot through me.

Four minutes since the last one had passed, I was told to come in straight away.

It was a struggle to dress. Mum helped me whilst Ken went out to warm the car.

Down to every three minutes, and the pain was so intense.

I'm sure Ken broke every speed limit to get me to the hospital. Mum sat in the back with me with one hand on my stomach, saying, 'Hold on... hold on,' every few minutes. The whole scene was like a comedy sketch.

Finally, we arrived, and by that time, I was a mess. The pain was unbearable. I forgot all of my breathing exercises from prenatal class—they went out the window—and I just could not think. The midwife, a lovely Oriental-looking lady, gave me some gas and air, and I floated!

Bring on the pain, now. I was in control.

There didn't seem to be a gap between contractions, and I hung onto the gas and air tube for dear life. I was attached to a monitor beside me, with numbers that increased when a contraction was detected. The midwife concentrated on the numbers and told Ken to get me to let go of the mask, but I would have none of it. I knew what I was feeling, and the numbers on the monitor were increasing rapidly. She kept saying, 'That's enough, now. Stop now. That's enough,' until her voice irritated the life out of me, and I screamed, 'GIVE ME THE F***ING GAS!'

The room became still. I opened my eyes to see my mother at the foot of the bed, mouth so wide open you could've fit a fist into it. I sighed and closed my eyes again, not being able to retrieve the cuss word that had escaped my vocal cords.

Mum picked up her bag, and as she turned, she snapped, 'I never knew Maria used words like that.' With that, she left the room. I felt bad, but the pain came again, and I took back my 'friend' and breathed the pain away as I floated into a legal high.

My midwife, Jan, bless her, was very patient with me. She had the most annoying, soft, baby-like voice that really started to grate on me. She smiled gently and began to encourage me, 'Now, Maria, you're nearly there. Think of it being a big poo and push.'

Was she for real?

I refused. What did she take me for? Why would I do such a thing?

She kept on and on till I thought if the poo was the barrier between my baby staying in or coming out, then so be it. If she wanted me to shit on the bed, then fine, and I pushed with all my might until I felt a huge release. I waited for an embarrassing smell to rise, but instead, I saw huge smiles from Jan and Ken.

He beamed. 'It's a girl.'

Huh!

I was confused. It was out? It was a girl? It was out?

Jan wrapped her and placed her in my arms. There, before me, was the cutest, dolly-faced baby, and I cried with happiness.

Ken went and got Mum. She still had a vexed face, but it soon melted when she saw her fifth granddaughter. All was forgotten, even the pain of childbirth. Three hours and 45 minutes, and there she was.

Nadia. Her name means 'the caller, the beginning, the first'.

My first baby. Our first. I was now a mummy at 19 years old, a teenager/young lady with a huge responsibility.

I was ready.

NEW BIRTH

Changes
Are we ever ready?
When our parents are too strict
You want to talk, but the atmosphere is thick
Best leave the boat to rock steady
No sense moaning about sitting alone
I wanted this
To feel like a woman loved
Now my womb is in bloom
But lonely in the days stuck in a bedsit room
I sigh
Rubbing my belly, I smile
New keys, and I have a place of my own

Dookie Dooks, look how far you've come
I didn't think you could be decently touched
And loved by a genuine man
What they did was meant to scar you
You don't fool me, though
I am you
And I feel everything you go through
I am a crying soul
Your inner me
Fighting off your enemy
Yes, all those untold memories
One man comes along
Singing a new song

Hypnotises you to think all wrongs have gone
But have they?

Push
Let that pain strangle your brain
Don't let those images stay to drive you insane
Push
With every contraction, let it be a distraction
Push
Oh, the pressure, the pain, the strain
Push
Again, again and again
Breathe in a methodical rhythm of Entonox
Float in another universe
Separate from the excitement
Loosen your body
Let it pass through
If I let go
You can let go, too
It is not just new life that disconnects from you
Push
You must
One last thrust
Push
All the pain of labour and the past

She's here, at last
What joy, the disbelief, you gasp
How can such excruciating pain birth happiness?

Your lover wipes your brow
Surely it will all be okay now
Breathe
The pushing has ceased
May the beauty of love increase
And your innermost find peace.

Chapter 12

TO HAVE AND TO HOLD

Nadia was my everything. I stayed at my parents' home for the first two weeks, and Mum pampered me. She did all the cooking; all I had to do was sleep, breastfeed and get used to motherhood. I had friends and family visit us during that time, and my bedroom looked like a florist's! Ken was besotted and displayed more love for me and Nadia. She was so small. She weighed six pounds, four and a half ounces at birth, which was a perfect size for a little newborn.

I moved into my new place after a few weeks had passed, and Ken also moved in. We were finally cohabitating as a cute little family, and I was more than happy.

Ken's son Daniel visited every other weekend, and in the summer, we all went to see Ken play his beloved sport of cricket if the weather wasn't too bad. There was a day we drove to take Daniel home, and as we journeyed back, Ken and I got into a conversation about life, our wants and desires and what we expected of our relationship. I loved speaking about the future. It all seemed like a fairy tale: me, Ken and Nadia, and no doubt, a couple more children. As a young teenager, I always imagined having five children because I felt like I wanted to form a happy bond like my siblings and I had once we'd grown up, but my children would be different. I would make sure they bonded properly and played nicely together from a very early age and have them close in age so one would not be spoilt over the others or teased and left out as I was. Ken wanted to get a degree in his field of work and eventually get a promotion. I wanted to return to work as a chef once Nadia was walking and talking. He also spoke of his parents looking forward to retirement in the West Indies, but their one desire was to see him settle down. They were really happy that we had become our own little family and seemed to be getting on quite well. His parents loved me, too. We got on rather well, and Ken and I visited them often, as well as spent time at his sister's and brother's respective homes; they were all married. Ken mentioned that his parents expected the same for him, and as we had Nadia, he didn't want to be anywhere else with anyone else but me.

Ken and I were on our way to my mum's when he suddenly pulled the car over. 'So, Maria, look—you know how I feel about you, and I want to make this more solid, especially to make my parents feel rested before they leave to retire. Your mum has also been making a lot of hints about us getting married, so how about it? Do you want to put up with me for a lifetime and get married?'

At 19 what did I know about proposals? I knew it should be some magical experience surrounded by romance, flowers and the man down on one knee, but this was Ken, the man who had taken my breath away and had my legs like jelly for months, the father of my first beloved child. How could I possibly say no? I remember the day as if it were yesterday. I sat in the car, literally speechless. I said yes, but it was a yes with disbelief that I'd heard correctly. Had he really asked me to marry him? I searched his face for clues, trying to read his emotions. Was this a serious talk, a real talk, just a chat talk, talking about his thoughts, or was he actually asking me? *Me!* Who would want to marry me? Was he having me on?

I felt immediately unworthy. Ken saw the doubt in me, too. He knew I struggled with self-confidence at times when it came to relationships due to my past.

Then, I heard his firm voice. It resonated down into my soul, which took the fear and disbelief away: 'I love you, Maria. Will you marry me?'

A smile broke out on my face, and my eyes filled with water. 'Yes. A hundred times, yes, of course, I'll marry you. I love you so much.'

Ken reached over to his glove compartment and took out a small box. He opened it, and there it was: the most beautiful gold diamond-cut ring with a single diamond in the centre. He'd planned this. He'd brought a ring with the intention to propose. He'd meant it.

Why would he spend money and go through so much trouble if he didn't want to do this? It was no act, this; right here, right now, was happening. It was one of the memories in my life that will never fade.

Ken placed the ring on my finger and kissed me gently but passionately.

Our parents were most excited at our news and marvelled at my ring. My mum looked somewhat relieved, and I'm sure it was the fact that I would no longer be a young lady with a child out of marriage. Although she loved Ken, deep down, she did not like our lifestyle, not that she was a church-goer, but she was set in her old-school ways.

Ken's parents were staunch Christians and attended church every week without fail, so they, too, were relieved and pleased. The wedding was set for later that same year to make sure Ken's parents would still be there before they flew back to the West Indies.

I spoke to the vicar of Mum's local church, which happened to be the same church my sister Cam and my brother Teddy were married in, and he was happy to do our ceremony.

I relied on Cam and Mum for input in all things. Ken was in charge of sorting out the reception, music and drinks. Our parents paid for the hall. There was no need for caterers back in those days. The best cooks in our family and friends were designated a dish to cook; just the basics in everything, no fancy table pieces, just a nicely decorated tabletop with gift savers at each table setting, which were normally gift-wrapped sweet almonds.

My cousin Shantel was to be my chief bridesmaid, and my niece, Cam's daughter, a bridesmaid. Ken's son Daniel was our pageboy, and my two little cousins, who were twin girls, were to be my flower girls. Mum and Cam went with me to a bridal boutique to try on some dresses and see what complimented me. The dress we all liked had a price tag that made us hold our breaths! We left smiling, knowing that Mum was going to make my dress, and she would add the gemstones and pearls to it, which were lacking in the dress I'd tried on. Cam's job was to make the bridesmaids' dresses; I was such a lucky girl to have two seamstresses in my family.

Over the months that followed, we fell into a nice routine and grew in our parenting, loving each moment with Nadia and filled with happiness at her growth and small milestones expected at her age.

My paternal grandfather passed away. I felt somewhat sad I guess. After all, he was still my granddad, but the news of his passing brought back memories of that indecent kiss and the fear I felt towards him afterwards. Questions arose yet again. Why would he have done such a wicked thing and abused the love I had for him?

There was an avalanche of stories that fell out of the closet after he died, and the true revelation of the life he lived was exposed. My poor grandmother was such a sweet woman, and to think she lived in a kind of bondage under the umbrella of her marriage made me sad. Granddad had done many sexually indecent acts as a spiritualist minister by 'anointing women's bodies with oils'! Well, you may think, what's wrong with that? It was the *kind* of anointing that was the problem.

Grandma had never travelled on a plane in her life, but my dad sent for her to come for my wedding. She was to come for three months to give her a well-needed break and for us to shower her with love. Everyone was excited about her pending arrival; she was loved dearly by all.

She arrived in time for Nadia's christening, which was a very small occasion, mostly because I've never believed in big parties for such holy events. The church was the same one we would use for our wedding. After the ceremony, we went back to my parents' home for refreshments. It was not a fancy affair, just our nearest and dearest.

Two months after the christening, it was to be my special day, the day I'd patiently waited for, and I would become Ken's wife. I was not just a 'baby mother', girlfriend or fiancé; I was about to have status. I knew of quite a few school friends who had babies but were in a boyfriend-girlfriend relationship, living separately. Most often, it was the girl who was still living at her parents' house.

The night before our big day, Ken left to be with his mates, and I stayed at Mum's. Bernel and Toni came over, and we had a girlie night, helping Cam and Mum hand-sew the last of the diamantes and pearls to the bodice of my bridal gown. The girls got ready to leave so I could settle down to sleep as I obviously had a huge day ahead and needed my rest, but how could I sleep? I was so anxious. I couldn't think. Would everything be okay? Then a frightful thought came: what if everyone forgot and didn't turn up?

I expressed my concerns to my sis, but Cam laughed and said we would still have a big party and eat all the food. I knew she was being funny, but the butterflies prevented me from laughing. Mum ushered me out of the room, told me everything would be just fine and to stop worrying, get to sleep and remember how happy I would be. Now, that made me smile. No sooner had my head hit the pillow than I was asleep.

My eyes opened with a burst of light through the curtain. It took me a few seconds to recollect my thoughts and realise that the day was the ninth of September, and the biggest grin lit my face as I bounced out of bed. Cam had stayed over, too, and I ran into her room, shaking her awake, giggling. She turned and smiled when she saw my excitement and said, 'Let the day begin.'

Bernel had taken Nadia with her the night before, and Ken was with his best man. We decided that we would not call each other under any circumstances unless there was an emergency with Nadia.

The first stop was the hairdresser's, and, as I feared, things started to go wrong. I stood in front of the locked door. I mean, the shutters were down, the door was locked, and I began to panic. Where was Donavon? We'd spoken about that day, the time I would come, the style I would have. Oh, and that was another thing: I forgot the tiara at home. He had told me to bring it along so he could style my hair around it. Oh, well. What could I do? I just had to wait. I mean, how late could he open up??? My appointment had been booked for 8.30 a.m., and there was Donavon, strolling towards me at 9.15 a.m. with a smile that told me he had no clue he was late.

'Hi, morning, darling. How yuh going? Have you been waiting long?'

I tried to breathe in a less frustrated rhythm as I answered, 'Don, we agreed 8.30, remember? It's my wedding day, and I've been a nervous wreck waiting for you.'

'Oh, shit! Oh, gosssh, Maria, I sorry, eh? Come, come. Farst, leh we do dis quick. Nah worry yuhself, girl. I clean forget.' Don's Grenadian accent sung through his excitement.

I smiled as we were now on the same page, and he knew my schedule. Well, a bride was meant to be late, right?

I called my brother, Curtis, to pick me up to save time on the train. He drove just over the speed limit to get me to Mum's to dress, but I had no complaints about his crazy driving at all.

Mum stopped me in my tracks as I raced through the front door, placed both hands on my arms and told me to stop and breathe, just breathe. I took a couple of deep breaths in and exhaled.

There. Calm.

We went upstairs, and I showered. It was refreshing, feeling the water cooling my skin, and I was somewhat relaxed once more. I sat on the stool for Mum to fix my hair with the tiara, and I did my makeup myself, I didn't want or need a lot.

When the dress was on, I turned to look in the mirror, and all I saw was a Black fairy tale princess. Mum's eyes sprung water, and I had to look away as I felt mine about to... but my makeup!

Ken's brother-in-law Elijah was my driver as he had a 7 Series BMW, but where was he? I was running late now, and the panic started to creep back into my nerves. Ken's sister Stella came running in, panting, saying that Elijah was stressed that the car needed washing — washing now? What the heck was really going on? I couldn't wait for the car to be washed and then fluffing around, trying to fit its ribbon. No, no!

I turned to my brother. 'Curtis, I beg you: use your car. It's 1.35, and the wedding should've started five minutes ago!

'Stella, wait here for Elijah and meet us at the church.'

Dad and I went in Curtis's car, and Mum drove her car with the bridesmaids. As we turned into the church gate, Curtis, in his fluster, crashed into the gate pole. No damage was done, but it was a scene out of a *Carry-On* film!

Hilarious.

The vicar was outside, waiting. We apologised, and he hurried us into the reception area, where we composed ourselves and my dress was smoothed out.

The organs started playing, and the doors opened. There, before me, was the longest aisle; each of the benches of seats was decorated with posies of flowers. I looked at the rows of seats, and there was hardly anyone there. I choked back tears, thinking people really had forgotten and didn't come.

I walked slowly down the aisle behind the flower girls, Ken's son Daniel and the bridesmaids, which felt like a long walk of shame. I smiled the tears away as the guests took pictures, gasped and smiled as I walked past them. I wanted to run, but I fixed my gaze on Ken, who looked the most handsome he had ever been, but in my mind, all I could think of was how empty the church looked. There would hardly be any wedding presents, and all the food would go to waste. This day could only go from bad to worse.

My mind was so preoccupied with these thoughts that the words of the vicar flew over my head like a soft breeze, but I do remember the vicar's voice raising as he proclaimed, 'As you have exchanged vows before God and witnesses, by the giving and receiving of rings, I now pronounce you husband and wife. You may kiss the bride.'

Ken raised my veil and kissed my lips tenderly, and I melted like I did the very first time he kissed me outside Panama's nightclub.

Everyone cheered. The sound made me look towards the guests, and I couldn't believe my eyes. The church was packed! I chuckled inside, and the relief was immeasurable. It was typical: Black people and timekeeping!

There was a short musical interlude as we signed the register, and after the vicar had said a few words, we turned to leave as Mr and Mrs Sajor.

The fake smile I'd had walking into the church, hiding my tears, was replaced by a huge grin, all of my teeth shining, holding Ken's hand and feeling like his queen.

The church had a beautiful garden, where we took all of our photos.

Elijah was waiting by the front of the church with the shiniest ribboned car that looked spectacular. Inside, between the back seats, there was a small pail with a bottle of Champagne on ice and two champagne glasses. We escaped the noise of the voices, the greetings, the extensive smiling as we journeyed on to the venue for the reception, I honestly thought my face would stick that way! I didn't realise how much being a bride had you as the centre of attention, and that was just the beginning.

The speeches were heartfelt, and my dad had a few dry jokes that everybody seemed to laugh at. Ken's uncle Sam's first words were to shout out, 'Ho made the saltfish? It was absolutely amazing.' My uncle had made it, and it was truly delicious. In fact, all of the food was amazing, and there was enough for everyone and more.

After we'd cut the cake and took more pictures, the tables were cleared, and a dance floor was made visible. Ken and I had our first dance, then everyone joined in.

The rest of the night was simply wonderful, with good music and lots of drinks. Ken did so well to sort that out with his brothers and his bonified group of friends.

The reception finished at 11 p.m., and Ken's best man and friend from school days Mark suggested an after-party back at our flat, so a group of friends and family gathered back at ours and partied until a little after 3 a.m. I had conked out by then; I was totally exhausted. What seemed to have started off as a disastrous day had soon been overturned into a glorious one.

Everyone eventually left, and Ken threw himself on the bed next to me, and we looked into each other's eyes. We both smiled in silent agreement. No wedding night specials that night! We fell asleep, cuddled up close and slept sound into the next day.

I awoke first, and the whole world felt brand new. I was new. Yesterday, I was Maria Skinner, but today, I awoke as Maria Sajor. I woke up Ken with breakfast in bed. I couldn't wait to go pick up Nadia and head to my parents' to open all of our gifts as I saw we had loads.

Ken had other ideas. He set the breakfast aside, reached over and caressed my body from my neck down to my toes. My mind slowed down as I became intoxicated by his touch. Our breathing escalated until eventually it could no longer be heard. There was silence; the only thing I heard was the friction of the silk sheets. I knew I was alive by the surrender of my body that danced in according to his.

Let the music play.

SHE SAID 'YES'

To be or not to be
Either be locked up in your inner me
Or rejoice in being set free
Can joy be found in rain?
The constant sound, pitter-patter
Increasing louder as it hits the windowpane
Joy knocking on the inner pain
Breaking down walls of shame
Let me go
Is it I who holds you, or you, me?
There is an exit door that lights the way for you to see
But your eyes are wide shut!
Still trying to figure out how to fight your enemy
It is, in fact, a memory
You have found love in your new family
A sweet love that beckons and asks politely, 'Marry me?'
Did I hear correctly?
You said yes wholeheartedly
Well, I'll be…
Footsteps walking out one…two…three
The day draws closer
It's the month of September
Heart tremors as you think no one remembers
Walking down the aisle wearing a watery smile
It is just life trying to steal your joy
Playing with your mind like a lifeless toy
Turnaround and see

The pews are filled with friends and family
Do not let your mind attack you so ferociously
Declare your vows, exchange your rings
Say I do and hear your heart and spirit sing
Embrace this next stage in life
Beware, it will not always be free of strife
To have and to hold until you grow old
Will be your greatest testimony
To be or not to be...
It is time to set yourself free
Now joined together in holy matrimony
To walk in fair weather between anniversaries
But remember the rain
Not every shower is a blessing
In your joy, be ready to face the pain
For in these times, you will need to press in
To be or not to be...
Real love is the key
Unlock your inner me
Sweetheart, love and be loved and set yourself free

Chapter 13

IT'S ALL ABOUT THE TEMPERATURE

Christmas was approaching, and it would be our first Christmas as a little family spent in our home. I was still at home, looking after Nadia while Ken worked. Money was a little tight, but we were coping. It wasn't as if we had to shop for three as Nadia was on baby food and formula milk, which was provided by milk tokens from the government. As for me and Ken, we did not eat that much portion-wise.

I was okay at home with my routine but lately, I had been getting tired during the day and by the evening I was so ratty that even Nadia got on my nerves. Ken and I started to have little snappy arguments. They weren't bad, but they sometimes had me on edge. I was off of my food, too. Mum said I was run down and didn't have a good diet. I was still breastfeeding in between, so it could be that my immune system was low. She urged me to go see my GP, hoping he would give me a prescription for some tonic or vitamins.

I did, and after I explained how I felt, he got the nurse to take my bloods. I took a urine test, and he advised me to drink plenty of water and rest.

The doctor called me back in later that day. I sat in his office as he turned to me and said I needed some tonic, not because I was rundown or anaemic, but because I was pregnant! My eyes shot wide open in shock. Looking back, all the signs were there: feeling nauseous in the evening, feeling ratty, being off my food, and lately, the metal taste in my mouth. He asked me if I was okay with that news. I smiled and said yes. He examined me, and judging by my dates, he estimated I was six weeks gone. I was given a couple of appointments, and he wrote up a letter to send to my preferred hospital, saying they would send me an antenatal appointment in the post. He said congratulations, and I left.

Walking out of the building, a million thoughts ran through my mind. Two children! What would Ken say? How would Mum and my friends react? Two babies in nappies! What would I do differently while in labour?

Labour! I smiled. In fact, I grinned and said out loud a delightful thought that sprung to mind' 'Gas and air, yes!'

Ken was at work; I was bursting to tell him. It was killing me to stay silent. The more I thought about it, the more I loved the fact another baby was growing within me.

I had composed myself. By the time he finally came home after his long day. I wanted to feel his mood. What if he wasn't as excited as me? He kissed me and said, 'Evening,' and I smiled. He knew something was up and asked if I had been to the GP.

'Yes, and he gave me his diagnosis this afternoon as he saw something—he saw a baby!'

Ken looked up. 'What?'

'You heard.' I smiled as I saw the twinkle in his eyes; his eyes always shone like diamonds when he smiled. He stood up, chuckled and kissed me. He joked saying that he now realised why I'd been so moody and snappy of late.

I told him the doctor said I was about six weeks, according to my menstrual cycle dates, so still in the very early days.

I wasn't one to keep news of a pregnancy until after 12 weeks pregnant, so I let my family and friends know I was expecting. After all, I was married now, so there was no shame in it. The feeling was so good, mentioning I was pregnant without fear of a backlash of negativity. Everyone we told was so happy for us, especially our parents. The thought of another little Nadia was pleasing to many as she was a beautiful baby in looks and temperament.

Christmas day was so lovely. In fact, it was beautiful. It was my first time cooking my very own Christmas dinner and serving it in the special silver dishes we'd received as our wedding gifts, and as I couldn't drink alcohol, we had apple Tango in our posh wedding champagne flutes. The best part of Christmas day was when Nadia took her first steps. It couldn't have been more perfect.

The weeks rolled into months; time seemed to fly by. My pregnancy was nothing like Nadia's. I grew as big as a whale. My hair was really healthy, and it grew, as did my feet, from a size five to a size seven! I waddled like a duck when I walked; it was quite comical. It was quite a hot summer, which didn't help. It was so different being heavily pregnant in the summer than in the winter, which I was before.

Ken left me at Mum's and took Nadia to drop Daniel off at a cricket match on the other side of London. I was alone, as everyone had gone to work. I was restless and decided to pop down to the shop for my much-craved-for pineapple juice, stopping off at the dry cleaners on the corner and chatting with the lovely couple that ran it. As we spoke, a sharp pain cut across my stomach, which winded me, and I doubled over. The lady, Mrs Bannerman, asked if I was okay as I composed myself. I said yes, it must've been a Braxton Hicks, although I thought it was rather strong to be that. No one was home, so I prolonged my conversation with them.

Seven minutes passed, and there it was again. Now, we all panicked as I doubled up and groaned. Mrs Bannerman got her husband to call my mum at work as she was closer than Ken was. Ken wasn't answering his phone, and I was sure that, although I was 38 weeks gestation, the baby was coming. It caught me off guard, as I expected it to be the same as my last experience.

As if my body had its own automatic alarm clock, the contraction came again. I held my breath involuntarily as the pain gripped me. Mr Bannerman tried calling Ken one last time, and by a miracle, Ken answered. Mr. Bannerman explained the situation, but Ken was too far for me to wait, and he decided it was best I get to the hospital, and he'd meet me there.

Mum was on her way. I had to get to the house to get my hospital bag, which was packed and ready and to call the labour ward. I waited for the last contraction to pass, and Mrs Bannerman slowly walked with me to our house. By the time we got to the house, Mum was pulling up, and I gave a sigh of relief at the sight of her.

Mum rushed into the house to grab my bag and quickly called the hospital. They were expecting us, and after I danced and rocked the next contraction away, we got going.

The labour was quick, and it seemed that Ken was going to miss the birth, as, after just a couple of hours, I was ready to push. Ken had rung to say he had dropped Nadia off at his sister's and would be right there.

I thought of where his sister lived and rolled my eyes. I looked at Mum, who was holding my hand and rubbing my back, and I fell into tears. I was scared. I wanted Ken. I needed to hear his voice and feel his touch. He always had a way of comforting me and saying the right words to make me feel safe. There were times when

I would have flashbacks of when we made love, images of indecent touches and accusing words that showered me with guilt, but Ken would hold me in his arms and gently kiss away the nightmares that tormented me.

Mum consoled and encouraged me as best as she could. After 20 long minutes, the door burst open. It was Ken. Oh, the relief.

I was ready to push. The gas and air made my head feel nice, but it was time to let go, to feel the urge to push with force (you gain wisdom and knowledge from your first labour!). My body trembled uncontrollably immediately after the baby came out, and it was all over. I heard the words, 'It's a boy!'

A boy! What did they mean? It must have been a mistake. My family doesn't have boys!! I panicked and burst into tears.

Ken was at a loss as to what was wrong, and I didn't want to hold the baby. There had to have been a mistake. He went out of the room to get my mum and tell her something was wrong.

She came rushing in. 'Maria, what is it? What's wrong?'

Sobbing, I explained, 'I don't know what to do with a boy. I've only ever had nieces, and my baby at home is a girl—why have I got a boy?'

Mum smiled and said, 'Well, darling, you only get two offers, male or female, and we take what's given and be thankful.'

I still didn't like it and spoke out my concerns. 'How do I put his nappy on. Is his little willy supposed to fit up or down in it? And how do I potty train—does he stand up or sit down? What if he misses?' I sobbed the words, and Ken and Mum did everything they could to suppress their laughter. Looking back, my concerns and fears were ridiculous and humorous, but they were so worrying to me at the time as having a boy felt so foreign to me.

The midwives, Mum, and Ken all comforted and reassured me that everything was going to be all right and celebrated the fact that this was the first grandson for my parents and the first nephew for my brothers and sisters. I smiled.

After I had calmed down, the midwife brought over the swaddled baby for me to hold. I looked down, and a burst of love covered me like a warm blanket. I kissed him as he slept.

As this was our first son, Ken named him. His name was Rishon, a Hebrew name meaning first boy. Ken had Daniel, of course, but Rishon was *our* first.

Again, I stayed at Mum's initially for some help, but only for two weeks, as it was more hectic having Nadia with me, as well. It was a little cramped, and I missed the comfort of our own home.

Things got back to normal quickly, and we slipped in our new routine well. Ken was having problems at work and began smoking a lot heavier. He stayed out longer and more often on Friday nights with the lads, which began to irritate me as I was no longer a part of that. I was now the stay-at-home mum with two young babies. It was upsetting as I hardly saw the girls, and I missed being able to go out clubbing, especially with my cousin Shantel.

Ken started bringing home his frustration from work. He was snappy, and we got into fits of shouting matches every other week. It was always a build-up until it blew up. The children would cry, which made me calm down, so they, too, would feel okay. Ken would slam the door shut as he went out for a smoke and a walk. He came back, and there would be silence. I would get the kids to bed, have a bath and go to bed myself. I would pour a small glass of straight rum and knock it back just to take the edge off the hurt and make sleep come faster. Those were the nights Ken came to bed and held me in his arms. There would be no words, but he would kiss me, and before I knew it, we were making love. That was his way of saying sorry. I was okay with it, as the rum helped the images stay away. I could get lost in oblivion and fall into a deep sleep afterwards, our bodies entwined and at peace.

We headed into difficult times financially. I wasn't working, just receiving Statutory Maternity Benefits and child benefits as income, which was very limited. Ken's salary was stretched, which did not make life any easier. He seemed to resent my staying at home even though we'd both agreed it was the best for the children. I resented him for resenting me. He constantly gave me the silent treatment, and I would flare up in anger as I hated his rejection of my touch or the lack of response when I tried to speak about my day and what the kids had done.

One evening, Ken was out of money and out of cigarettes and the cupboards were bare except for the things to make breakfast, but it was dinner time! I made scrambled eggs, bacon and baked beans. It wasn't a meal expected in the evening, but it was food, and it was hot. The kids had already eaten, bathed and were in bed.

I made the meal in silence, fed up with the atmosphere in our home. I didn't like it. It wasn't us. Every time I spoke to Ken, he grunted a response, and I was getting so frustrated and angry. 'For crying out loud, Ken, your situation at work isn't my fault. Stop damn well taking it out on me.'

No response.

'Ken, I'm talking to you—why won't you lis—'

Before I could get the whole word out and finish my sentence, he got up in a fit of rage, flung his plate at me and shouted, 'SHUT UP, SHUT UP!'

I turned to get out of the way, but the plate smacked me on the back of my head, and I dropped to the floor. The next thing I knew, I felt warm water trickling over my face. Ken's voice mumbled, 'Look what you made me do.'

Look what I made *him* do?! I felt dazed, and then it sunk in: I had been knocked out. Ken had never hit me before. My mind swirled with thoughts. I felt so confused, and then a wet warmth brought me back to reality. He'd knocked me out, but he loved me, I reasoned with myself.

I knew he loved me; he'd used warm water to wake me up and not cold. Ken knew how much I hated cold water on my skin. Surely, he cared enough, loved me enough, if he used warm water, didn't he?

I looked up, and the tears rolled down my face in silence. I didn't—couldn't—say anything, and Ken seemed too ashamed to. I got up slowly, looked at him and brushed past him. There were baked beans and eggs in my hair. I wanted a bath, a hot bath, to wash away the pain. Yes, not the food, the pain.

What the heck had just happened? What was happening to us? Had we resorted to this?

I ran the water. My eyes blurred. The bathroom was steamy. I stripped off my clothes and stepped slowly into the bath, one leg at a time. It was scalding. Once that leg had adjusted to the heat, I put in my other leg and stood there, held onto the sides of the bath and slowly bent my legs to immerse myself in the hot water. I couldn't feel how hot it was; I was numb. As I sat there, I mumbled, 'He'd used warm water. He loves me. Yes, he loves me. Of course, he loves me. He used warm water. I'm his wife. He asked me to marry him. I never forced him. He used warm water. Yes, he loves me. He didn't use cold water. He used warm water...' And so the mumbling continued whilst I sat in water that was too hot for me to be able to move. I needed the burning to distract my mind, numb me.

I slipped down into the water once it was bearable and drifted off to sleep. I was awoken by Ken, I don't know how long after I'd dropped off, but the water was lukewarm, and the back of my head was wet. He called out my name and shook me.

At first, I'd forgotten what had happened, but it came back. I looked at him blankly, reached for my towel and got out of the bath. I had no words, no energy to dry my skin. My towelled dressing gown was hanging on the back of our bedroom door, and I reached for it, put it on, wrapped it around me, crawled into bed and curled up like a foetus.

There would be no intimacy that night to apologise. My thoughts swirled. Seven repeated words wooed me to sleep. 'He Used Warm Water. He Loves Me.'

THE FLOWER CALLED LOVE

A seed was sown
It's down deep in the soil below
When it was sown, I do not know
But it was watered and fed
And arisen from the soil bed.
Wait, it's okay, for I see a bud
I assume it is a darling bud of May
A blossom of sweet fragrance of love
Potentially to form a bouquet
Presented to one's lover on Mother's or Valentine's days.
Out from the stem, thorns take form
The aesthetic senses, perfume and colours that radiate sunset red
Intoxicating my head
But instead of imitating life, Dookie Dooks feels dead
There is a change in climate
Winds begin to twirl and rise
Her life is about to change before her eyes
Scalding hot baths and tears that stream silently down her face

I'm sorry
I didn't forewarn you
Falling head over heels in love
Fearing not the trials of life
And how a lack of money can bring on stress and strife
The hand that says sorry touches by caress
In your heart, I made you feel everything was blessed
Here lies the greatest test

Alison Ryan -Chase

Will you stay and endure
So all will see a perfect love?
Or will you go and save/change your life?
No, of course, you'll stay
You have learnt over the years
To wear a mask called 'everything is okay'
What can I say?
What can I do?
I want to try and save you
But your love for him is strong and true
And even though he knocked you out
He does, in fact, love you, too
Even though it was a heavy clout
Your eyes opened
And so did your mind
But instead of the truth, I whispered into your heart
The water—remember the water
The care he took to wash your face and hair
It was not cold but rather warm
So, no matter the reality of the storm that just brewed
No matter what I can whisper
To deliver you from what's sure to come after
No matter the warning signs
All that matters in your life is Ken, Nadia and Rishon
You are determined to carry on
As far as you are concerned
You must have caused the situation
After all, that's what was said
I should've told you; you could've dropped dead

A seed was sown
Out of the fertile soil grew a rose
It spelt love and grace, joy and peace
You held it, not knowing the pain it could release
Warm water...
It grew with warm water
As long as you held the rose between the thorns
It was capable of giving love and not hurting you
Beauty that deceived
You left your parents to cleave
No way will you entertain the words to leave
So, what did I do?
I left you to believe
Because he used warm water,
He loved you

Chapter 14

WHEN PASSIONS OVERFLOW

It took a few weeks for Ken and me to start talking again. With him, it was due to shame and guilt. I was upset as I was the victim, even though, to be honest, I missed sharing the love we had.

Friends came over to visit one evening, and that's what broke the ice. It was hard to put on a mask and stay vexed afterwards. The children were such good playmates, and they played well in the playgroup I took them to every Thursday.

A new nursery opened in the area that was taking on children with sibling discounts. I registered Nadia and Rishon, and thankfully, they were accepted. Ken's work colleague, who was giving him a hard time, was dismissed, and Ken had a promotion, so things were a little easier. Ken and I decided that it was a good time for me to go back to work. I was accepted for the first application and job interview I made, and the hours were perfect to fit around the children's schedules. Things were more than good; they were great. Ken and I had put the plate incident behind us. Being freshly married had its ups and downs whilst finding your feet, and we just considered that blip to be one of our downs.

Everyone saw us as the perfect little family. We looked great as a couple, our children were beautiful, and our home was always welcoming. Valentine's Day, Mother's Day and my birthday were three of my favourite days of the year, as during them, I was always showered with love. Ken spoilt me, and I spoilt him double. We were comfortable in our routine, and my going back to work, his promotion and the kids settling at the nursery were blessings.

Christmas was around the corner, and we decided to spend it with our parents. The family enjoyed seeing our kids, and it was a time when all the little cousins met up.

Work was tiring in the weeks leading up to Christmas due to the dropping off of the kids, the commute to work, standing up all day cooking, then journeying back again, which had my eating times out of whack. By the evening, I just couldn't face eating. I was glad when Christmas day came as I didn't have to do one thing but get myself and the kids ready, which Ken helped me with.

Our first stop was Ken's parents. They were so happy to see their grandchildren. His sister and her family were there, too. We didn't eat much or stay very long as we still had to drive down to my parents afterwards.

Mum, as usual, cooked up a storm; her traditional Trinidadian Christmas dinner and her freshly baked breads, cakes and sweetbread made the day so special. Maybe it was due to eating breakfast late and then dinner (although it was light) at Ken's parents' but I couldn't eat a lot and was quite tired. Mum looked at me. 'What you mean you're not hungry? You come all the way here and not eating good food? What happen? Yuh pregnant or something?' She chuckled, and everyone in earshot laughed.

I smiled and said that I was just over full, but inside me, a light bulb flickered on. So fast? Pregnant? No way. But my mind looked swiftly back at myself over the past few weeks.

No, no! It wasn't possible, anyway. Yes, we were both forgetful when it came to birth control, but I was taking it regardless. As for my menstrual cycle, it was as irregular as our local bus! I got myself a test to put my mind at ease. As my morning sickness was always in the evening, I told myself that I would see if I felt overly tired that night and in the evening the day after. There was no need to panic just yet. Obviously, I was tired and feeling a little off, but there was still the next day.

Boxing day we stayed over at Mum's as Ken had had a few drinks, and the kids had had a late-night playing. During the day, I clean forgot about checking myself and had a lovely relaxing day after the excitement of Christmas.

Before long, tiredness came upon me. Mum offered me food but I couldn't, and the only drink I fancied was a sip of water. Maybe I'd eaten something bad or had the stomach flu. Then my eyes popped wide open, and I looked at the time. It was 5 p.m. I gulped. I'm not sure if the words, 'Oh, shit,' were audible or if I said it in my mind; it was Boxing Day. All the shops closed early, so there was no going to the pharmacy until the next day. It was going to be a long night.

Mum and Dad encouraged us to spend another night, and I was happy for the extra pair of hands with the children, especially feeling the way I did.

As soon as I woke up the next day, I had a shower and went down to the shops at the bottom of the road. I brought something to hide the Clearblue Pregnancy test I got at the pharmacy.

I hurried back. Everyone was preoccupied and didn't notice my movements. I headed to the bathroom, locked the door, breathed in, slowly exhaled, then began to take the test.

The cross was crystal clear: I was pregnant.

What would Ken say? My mum? My friends? Baby number three. Three children under five. Wow!

I know we'd wanted children, but they were popping out pretty fast. I was happy yet nervous. The thought of gas and air didn't quite cut it that time. Ken and I were getting on like in the early days of our relationship, I was working, and our lifestyle was comfortable. What would he say? I needed a cushion to soften the blow of his words. I thought it best to say something now while we were in Mum's company.

I went downstairs. The kids were playing happily with their new toys, and Ken was chatting to Mum and Cam, who had popped in. My sister had a huge smile as she said hello to me, and I forced a smile back. I couldn't hide my nervousness. Cam searched my face and asked what was wrong. Why did I look like I had lost a pot of gold? With a half-smile I said that I hadn't lost anything. It was more like I'd found something.

I turned to Ken, actually wishing I could retract my words and just hide a while longer. 'Ken, I know this may not be the best of times, but I've just found out that our family is about to get bigger.'

Ken looked bewildered. It wasn't until Mum's and Cam's reactions that he caught on. 'Maria, oh, my gosh. THREE!'

Cam blurted out, 'Well, girl, yuh good not me mate, but you and Ken cope well, so what's one more?'

Mum looked amused and quipped, 'Ken, yuh real have my daughter busy.' She giggled and said that all children were blessings and gave us her congratulations.

Ken still seemed out of sorts. He looked at me and said, 'Now, that's a Christmas surprise present. Oh, my God—three! How the heck... well girl, we just gotta deal with it. It will be okay.' He reached over, kissed me, and rubbed my belly as he sighed. 'Baby number three, huh? Okay.' He smiled, bowed his head for a minute or so then rubbed it. He turned and looked at Nadia and

Rishon. 'Roll on the new year!' He glanced over at me with a reassuring expression and that was what made me exhale after holding a very long breath. It was what I needed. Now, I could relax. Hey, I was married, and that's what married people do, have children, right?!

Then, why did I feel so awkward telling people? Their responses were more or less the same which made me feel so embarrassed for being pregnant again. 'Three kids?!'

Yes, three. What the heck? I wasn't a baby mama with three different baby daddies.

I just smirked along with them and replied, 'Yeah, me and my husband will have three.'

My pregnancy was the same as with Rishon, and I swore I was having another boy. By that time, I didn't mind if it was a boy or a girl. Well, actually, I secretly wanted a boy to keep Rishon company as he was surrounded by girls.

I worked up until my seventh month, then went on maternity leave, but I knew I wasn't going back in three months. I needed time with my baby, time for it to grow big enough to express his like or dislike for childcare when I eventually went back to work. Maternity leave meant maternity pay, which was much lower than my salary. We had to make cutbacks, which made Ken a little on edge at times. He wasn't the greatest at dealing with change, especially when there was a decline in finances. There were bouts of bickering between us, but not to the extent where it got physical.

Ken and I moved from the temporary accommodation to a short-term council accommodation. It was a two-bed flat on the ground floor on the outside border of a local estate. We were so happy not to be in a high rise. There wasn't a back garden, but we did have a small front garden; it was home.

It was the middle of summer, and Ken had gone to cricket. Some weekends, we went along for the day, but I was near my due date, and running after Nadia and Rishon was not the one. I decided to stay and cook a really nice Sunday dinner. I fancied some callaloo, macaroni pie, stew boiler chicken and rice 'n' peas. Cam and her husband, Patrick, passed by to see if I was okay and drop off some of Patrick's vegetables from his allotment. We had a laugh, and they asked if I needed anything before they left, but I was fine. We said our goodbyes, and they hugged and kissed the kids, who began to cry as they left through the front door. Patrick's heart went soft, and he said they'd take them for a few hours so I could chill. Inside, I leapt in joy. I quickly got a bag sorted for them, and off they went.

It wasn't even five minutes after they left that I felt as if I was peeing myself. I ran to the toilet, but just a trickle came out. This was part of the pregnancy I hated, feeling as if I were bursting because I needed to pee but only a little came out, nothing close to what I expected. I needed to change my underwear, but as soon as I got up, I trickled again. Guessing the baby was resting on my bladder, I decided to put on a sanitary towel as I wasn't going to change knickers every few minutes. Before long, the pad was soaked. When I went to change it, I saw a plug of mucus, but there was no streak of blood. I was confused.

Just then, the phone rang. It was my auntie Ann, who was a midwife—what were the chances of that stroke of luck? After I'd told her what was happening, she said it seemed like my waters had broken. I imagined it would have been a big gush when that happened, as my waters had always been broken by the midwives in my past labours. I told her I wasn't in any pain, too embarrassed to ask if the waters came out of the same place as my wee; well, they never told us in prenatal classes! She told me to put another pad on so the midwives could see and measure how much of my waters had gone and to ring the labour ward to let them know.

Here we go again, I thought.

Why had it not happened while Cam was there, for Pete's sake?

I reached for the phone again to call the cricket club, but I was stopped in my tracks by a pain that shot across my stomach. Before long, Ken arrived, and we left straight away as the pain was getting intense, and the water was coming down faster. It was not at all what I imagined it to be.

After two labours, I must have been immune to the gas and air as it wasn't working. In addition to that, the midwife offered me Pethidine, which I gladly accepted. Ken said he had just hit a six when Terry, the barman, came running across the pitch, waving and shouting: 'KEN… KEN… HER WATERS 'AV BROKEN!' It sounded so comical that I couldn't hold back the laughter. I thought it must've been hysterical.

I was well-behaved in this labour. It was relatively calm. Before I knew it, after two more big pushes, our second son was born. Ken named him Ethan, which means firm and strong. He was little, but he had a firm grip and looked like a right little wrestler. Ken was happy. He adored all his children and was an excellent dad.

I loved Ken, but when we argued, anger stirred in me to boiling point, and I would have a fit of rage and lash out. All I wanted was a happy marriage, a happy home, a man to call my husband, a devoted husband who cherished his wife. I'm somebody's child, and surely, I deserve to be treated right. Why couldn't he see the damage he was causing? Why couldn't my life be like the *Cosby Show*? That couple loved each other. Yes, it was a show on TV, but when Ken and I were out with family and friends, that's who they compared us to. We were a shining example of a good, young family.

Our life fell into a cycle that started with Ken being silent. I would get in a strop as I hated the atmosphere his silence caused in the house. I would then start to do the dishes but loudly. I banged everything in frustration and slammed the kitchen cupboards with hot tears behind my eyes. Why did we have to be like that? Why couldn't we be a normal, happy, loving family? Where was my fairy tale? It was not what I envisioned. I felt like I was a caged bird who had lost her voice, no longer having a sweet song to tweet but rather a quiet groan from deep within. It wasn't a nice environment.

The children also seemed on edge, and Rishon cried for every little thing. My banging caused Ken to start cursing and go out for a smoke. He'd come back in, and I'd start, 'What's wrong with you? Why won't you speak to me? What did I do?' All I got was the silent treatment, and my temper was engulfed in flames of shouting and screaming, and then came the floods of tears. What was happening to me, to us?

Ken would eventually realise I'd gone over the edge and take care of the children and get them ready for bed. He would read them a bedtime story while I sat in the kitchen, feeling deflated, with a bottle of wine. I felt useless, and I was failing, but failure was not an option. Our marriage had to and would work.

It was after those outbreaks that Ken would come to bed, and it seemed his version of being sorry was to be intimate. My mind, however, had grown an army, and the battle was real. It was a fight to separate reality from my nightmare memories buried in the depths of my soul, visions of hands touching me, and I could identify each hand without seeing the face. I opened my eyes to look at Ken to keep me in the present, but it still didn't help as I felt too ashamed to see what we were doing.

I felt dirty every time. How I had three children was beyond me, as sex was difficult most of the time. Ken could feel it when I clammed up, which I know annoyed him. He kept telling me it was okay, that it was him, but the scars were real, and they occasionally bled.

It was customary that after making love, I got up to take a hot bath. My hips were in excruciating pain, not because Ken was rough with me but my joints seemed to ache so much since having Ethan. The old pain in my knee came back after many years of being dormant, and the bath seemed to calm everything down and relax me from the turmoil I had gone through.

By the time I got back to bed, Ken was fast asleep, snoring. I climbed back into bed and wrapped my body around his. He nestled himself into me so we fit together like pieces of a jigsaw puzzle, and sleep came.

That was the peace I needed and craved. When I had it, I grabbed it with both hands, and it stayed until the next time Ken had a bad day at work and came home with the mood that started the ticking bomb of events. I knew what would happen. What always happened.

Ethan turned 12 weeks, and was growing well. Even though there were far too many arguments between Ken and I, Nadia and Rishon were such joyful children. They played together so well and they loved their baby brother.

Ken came home from work. He looked tired, but he was in a relatively good mood. There was no easy way to tell him. He looked at me and saw something was up.

'What is it, Maria? What's happened? The kids okay?' I reached into my pocket, took out a white stick and opened my hand to reveal it in its entirety.

There it was: a cross!

He looked at me, startled, flopped down into the chair and said, 'F***ing hell, no way.'

KALEIDOSCOPE LOVE

Fireworks
No, not the kind on the Fourth of July
Or celebrations to mark a brand new year
No colourful lights to light the sky
It's an explosion of emotions that brings heartfelt tears
How is it possible for love to cascade
Down a steep rocky slope?
Diminishing any resemblance of hope
In my mind, my heart, I simply cannot cope

Silence fills the air.
I think and wonder...
When was the last time I sensed he cared?
Awww... warm water! Oh, yeah
You see, my Dookie Dooks
Love is still in the air
When you start doubting,
Go back to the night when baked beans and eggs filled your hair

I've tried so many times to show you
To remind you how men are
But you used all your energy to cover up those rigid scars
What do I do? What can I do?
For richer, for poorer
In sickness and in health
What really did I mean when I vowed for better, for worse?
Did I, in fact, decree a curse?

Alison Ryan -Chase

The unbearable silence
Words spat in hate
Anger, bitterness and resentment formed an alliance
And now the marriage is in a hideous state
And yet
In the times of despair, to show that he cared
His lips kissed gently in the midnight hour
He touched you softly until you couldn't breathe
You forgave him with so much ease
Fighting through nightmares, so wanting to please
I knocked on the door to your mind, but you declined to answer
I could see from inside, tumours of pain formed like cancer
Ready to destroy anything good
Your hunger to be loved so misunderstood
How you define love
To others, it would sound insane
Yet the penetration of his kind of love
Has you pregnant again!... and again...
Shhhh, I hear you say to me
Stop being so fearful of what the future has in store for me
Should I be worried filling my womb again after three?

Yes, Dookie
You're about to see
And face a cruel reality
Regardless of whether you are married or not
You've conceived in the midst of hardship and strife
People will not consider you as a wife
As you'll be forced to consider an abortionist's knife

I am here
Always here
And I will hug you internally
A new nightmare is about to arise
Words shall cover truth with lies
For every child gifted to you is a blessing
Unfortunately, you and Ken will not realise
And darkness awaits with tears in your eyes
Fireworks so loud it deafens your ear
Your inner me crying out but no sound do you hear
No one is speaking to you intellectually
I ask… What is this pregnancy's contingency?

Chapter 15

NINE AND
A HALF WEEKS

Ethan was only three months old when I found out I was pregnant again. If I thought it was tough with three under five, there were about to be four under five. This baby and Ethan would be the same age at some point during the year, as they would be less than a year apart.

I wanted to scream. This was the first pregnancy where there were no smiles and no excitement. I was scared. What was in Ken's mind? I just needed to leave him alone for a while to breathe and take it all in. All I needed was his approval, something that said, 'I love you. We can do this together, and I'll be okay with it all.' I just wanted his support, and then I could fight the world. After all, he'd helped make it!

Never in my life did I think abortion would be an option in my life. It was for single people, people who were in a difficult situation in their pregnancies, like being deserted by their partners or raped, but I was married. Through all our arguments, I loved Ken, loved our little family, loved being a wife and mother.

Talking of mothers, my mum was most concerned. Her first response was, 'Maria, you simply can't go through with this pregnancy. Ken is struggling to make ends meet. You can't breathe and just about manage with the three you have. You have no choice—get rid of it,' just like that: no emotion, no concern. It flew out of her mouth as fast as oxygen flowing out of her lungs. Tears welled in my eyes, and I turned to look at Ken's reaction, but his head was bowed low, and he said nothing! What did his silence mean?

I found my words in the whirlwind of emotions. 'But it's killing a baby. My baby. The children's brother or sister. What will I say? How will I explain the reason for putting this baby to sleep if I get pregnant in the future?' The tears broke through the barrier of my lashes and streamed down my face.

Mum intervened. 'Maria, catch yourself. Number one, it is not a baby. It is a mass of cells still. Surely, you can see the strain and pressure Ken is under, and it will get worse. You're young. You have time to have another child in the future, but not THIS YEAR! Nursery runs, breastfeeding and looking after Ethan… it's cruelty. No, Maria. My advice to you and Ken is to get rid of it.'

Under my skin, it grew hot like fire with anger, not just at Mum's words but at Ken just sitting there, not defending his unborn baby or me. I could've boxed his lights out, but Mum was there, and no way was I going to show her the other side of us. For me, it was important that she saw at least one of her children's marriages work. Cam's first marriage had ended in divorce; my eldest brother Teddy was now divorced after just five years, and my other brother Lincoln's marriage was on the rocks but more visible than ours. Gosh, someone's marriage had to work!

Mum turned to Ken. 'Well, what you think, Ken, as this involves you, too? I stated my feelings on this predicament with you in mind. You feel you can handle a baby... another baby?'

He rubbed his hands over his face as if he'd just woken up. 'Look, whatever Maria decides, I will stand by her.' Now, what the heck was that supposed to mean? What a cop-out. How was that supporting me? How did that put a bandage over the cuts from Mum's tongue? He had mouth enough to cuss and carry on when we disagreed on things, yet the minute I truly needed him just to love me through a difficult situation he couldn't—or wouldn't—show any strength or control. 'I will stand by her!!!'

I sat there, unable to speak anymore. Mum got up and said she needed to go but to think very hard and quickly as the last thing we wanted was to make this linger until it became noticeable. And with that, she left.

I was numb. I couldn't look at Ken as I blamed him. I'm not sure what for—maybe all of it, but it felt easier to blame someone else, and I was hurt that he hadn't spoken up more.

I looked at the pregnancy book that had been given to me by the prenatal clinic in hospital when I was pregnant with Nadia. It was so cool. It showed a week-by-week of the baby's growth up to the fortieth week with illustrations. A group of cells; not a baby, Mum had said, but at nine weeks, there was a visible heartbeat, according to the book. I was at six weeks. If I were going to go through with it, I would have to think and act fast, but the pressure… I felt so much pressure I couldn't think straight, and all Ken would say was that he would support anything I decided. The more I heard those words in my mind, the more upset I got. I knew full well that if I chose to continue with the pregnancy, I would be blamed for all the setbacks, all the hardship, all the debt, everything bad. How on earth could I do something I've never agreed with my whole life? The only thing keeping me sane was that it needed to be done before I was nine weeks!

I booked to see my GP the following day. He was very nice and sympathetic after hearing the reasons why I was heading down the path of putting my baby to sleep (I couldn't say the words 'killing' or 'abortion'. They felt cold, heartless, like cuss words.). He gave me a referral letter to a Marie Stopes abortion clinic. The whole process seemed so long, and it seemed as if no one cared about the time frame but me.

It was just over a week that I had to wait for the appointment, which was more of a consultation. The therapist spoke at length, trying to get a sense of my mental well-being. All of it was pointless. What did it matter? It wasn't like I had much choice in the matter. Mum was adamant the baby had to go. Ken was on the fence, but only because he was too gutless to speak up. He did, however, say that he didn't want to say yes in agreement with Mum as he didn't want me to blame him, but I already did!

The day came for the procedure. Ken drove me there, but he couldn't stay as he had Ethan. Nadia and Rishon were at nursery. There were two other women in the waiting room. One was a young teenager who was as tearful as I was and who looked awfully scared. The other was a young woman, maybe in her late twenties, with her partner. They sat holding hands, and I couldn't help but wonder what their story was.

'Maria Sajor.' My name was called, but it sounded like a distant echo underwater. I was shaky when I stood up, and tears burned my eyes. What was I doing? It was my body, my baby—okay, cells; it was just a mass of stuff. I had to fill my mind with a vision of cells as I lay on the bed. A nurse spoke to me, telling me what to expect and asked if someone was coming to collect me as I couldn't go home on my own. I whispered, 'Yes,' and sobbed. She rubbed my arms and said that everything would be all right. Before giving me the anaesthetic, she asked if I was sure this was what I wanted. It was like giving last rites. I nodded my head shamefully as she started to give me the injection. I heard the surgeon read my file, asking me to confirm my name and date of birth. I said yes to all.

I felt a sharp scratch, and cold fluid entered the vein in my hand. I heard, 'Young woman, 23 years old, nine and a half weeks gestation, marr—' And everything went black.

I screamed 'Stop!' in my mind, and my eyes opened. Thank God, they'd heard me. Where was the nurse? She was just there. I had a baby, not cells. Nine and a half weeks. That meant I had a baby, not cells. It had a heartbeat, according to my book, so no, I couldn't put my baby to sleep. Everyone would have to understand.

The nurse came out from around the curtain, and I smiled at her. 'How are you, Maria?

'Everything went well. We'll give you a couple hours to make sure there are no after-effects, and you can call the person who is to collect you.' I lay there, gobsmacked, but I just blinked my eyes. What did she mean?

'I don't understand. I cried out to stop. I thought you heard me. What do you mean? I just shut my eyes for a second.' I sobbed as she explained the effects of the anaesthetic, that when I'd spoken out, it was in my mind as I'd gone under within seconds.

'But my baby... I was nine and a half weeks. It had a heartbeat. Was it a boy or a girl?' I was inconsolable as I hadn't realised, with all the appointments I had gone to, time had slipped by, and I'd lost count.

I'd put my baby to sleep. It was gone, and the pain was intense, the same afterpain as with delivering a baby. My stomach was contracting. It was the most horrendous pain. I felt like I was going to die. Was God punishing me for murder?

The nurse gave me a shot of Pethidine... I think that's what she said it was—I was too upset to hear her words, and I drifted into sleep.

Weeks and months passed, and my life was a cloud. My joy for Ethan had been stripped away with the loss of my baby. Yes, MY baby; nobody else wanted it except for me. Mum tried to make it seem right, telling me that God would understand, He would not punish me, and it was for the best for both me and Ken. Oh, my gosh, it was just too much. Sometimes, I cried without realising it. I'd blink, and there were tears. I had to pull myself together for the kids' sakes, and I hated crying in front of them.

I constantly heard a newborn baby crying in the night while I slept, and in the quiet times of the day, but when I got up to look, there was no baby. I was going out of my mind. Butterflies fluttered in my stomach. It was the same feeling as the first kick you get from your baby in the womb. Then, the thoughts started: what if they left a part of the baby in me? What was making that movement? It was a constant, daily reminder of what I'd done.

Nine and a half weeks.

I'd gone over the cut-off time I'd given myself so I wouldn't stop a heartbeat—how awful that I would have to live with that for the rest of my life.

Ken was true to his word. In the months following, he was very supportive and cradled me in his arms when I needed it. He tidied up and cooked when I couldn't. There was no fighting or arguing. To be honest, I wouldn't know how. Ken loved on me, and one day, he said that if he'd known it would have affected me so badly, he would've never let me go through with it. I was glad he'd said it, but it was too late.

Alison Ryan -Chase

THE PAIN OF FERTILITY

Aaaaaarrrrgghhh
What am I to do?
There's no getting through to you
For every spoken sore, there is a plaster
Useless tears that fill a carving of alabaster
A long bandage of reasons,
To kill the life within me is treason
Betraying the care given unto me
Entrusted to nurture,
Yet trouble and strife
Is all they envision
Am I then living and seeing a delusion?
I am but an emptying jug
Cascading out to a river of confusion
Shall I tell myself the inner wall of my womb holds an illusion?

Dookie
I'm so sorry
I couldn't find the right words to shout
And make your mother's words turn like a roundabout 360!
I know you thought being married would be your curtain
A covering that would shield you from indignation
You looked to him to defend
He said for better for worse
Yet when you needed him, he abstained from putting you first.

If I could just let you know
That your inner me intercedes for you
Crying out, your spirit begs for mercy and grace
But it is not time yet for you to understand
How much your unborn child is in HIS hands
You've catapulted into deep misery
Fighting demons day and night
Crying babies that are out of sight
I wish I could save you from this despair
Through it all
Love has evolved
He covers you with a marital shawl
His affection awakened, trying to help you stand up
Sounds of laughter from your sons and daughter
Helps the sadness take shelter
Out of hibernation, of guilt and self-hate
Enough — it's time to recuperate
Come out of this depressive state before it is too late

Oh, my baby, how I adore you
Your tiny hands
Your cute little face
My imagination goes crazy
Picturing what you would have looked like
And whether you were a boy or a girl
I'm so sorry
So very, very sorry
But it was out of my control
I couldn't win in the blame game

Looking back, I feel so ashamed
That when I came under attack
I had no backbone for you to fight back
Who knows? I could have won
And all the naysayers shocked and surprised
As they never realised that you'd grow to be the exceptional one

I'm sorry I put you to sleep, beloved
If only you knew how much I suffered after
Crying over a baby I never knew
Always remember, my precious
As you lay in the hands of Jesus
Mummy did, and always will, love you

Chapter 16

HOME SWEET HOME

It was a little over a year before the intensity of the nightmares from that trauma subsided. I still heard newborn babies crying in the wind, but it didn't torment me as it had before.

After the procedure, I decided on the Depo-Provera injection as a contraceptive. It needed to be administered once every three months, which suited me just fine. Plus, it stopped my monthly cycles.

Ken really looked after me. I know he'd felt it, too, and the only way he seemed able to cope with the loss was by diving into caring for me and the kids. He was such a good dad. The children screamed in delight every time he put the key in the lock when he came home from work. The first thing he did was drop his keys, take off his jacket and drop to the floor to give them horseback rides. There was always a mad fit of giggles. Everything was great, I guess.

In the summer, we spent most of our Saturdays down at the local cricket club watching Ken play. I even started making cricket teas for the players and learnt how to score. Things were hard, but we were comfortable and went with the flow of life.

I occasionally went out with Bernel, Toni and Kacee, and Ken went to see his crew every other Friday. It was what kept us sane and made us feel like we were still young and could have some fun outside of our four walls.

The apartment was becoming claustrophobic as the children got bigger and accumulated more toys. We decided to go ahead and buy our own house with the help of a grant from the local council. It put a pep in my step—finally, more of my dreams were coming true. I was married and now a prospective homeowner. It made me feel so mature over my peers. I had a proper little family—imagine me: an actual homeowner.

Obtaining a mortgage was quite stressful, but we finally got one. Ken had a friend who worked in finance. He told us which companies didn't do credit checks using systems that would pick up our previous bad credit results.

Looking at houses was so much fun, but the stress came when they all fell through, one after another. Either the other party in the chain pulled out, another buyer offered more or the surveyors disapproved of the worth of the property.

Finally, we found our dream house, a three-bedroom with a fitted kitchen, a bathroom, bedrooms and two fireplaces, one in the sitting room and the other in the dining room. The garden was huge, with a swing for the children and a garage at the end of it.

I went back to work to help with our income and to get out of the house to interact with other adults for a change. Ethan was with a lovely childminder who didn't cost an arm and a leg. Nadia started school, and Rishon was in nursery. Our family was stable, and life was good.

After a couple of years at home, I got a job in a private daycare nursery. The hours were ideal, working around our children's school hours. By then, they were finally all going to the same school, and our routine was very straightforward.

My duties at work were to create menus and cook lunch and afternoon tea for children aged three months to five years old and the staff team. It was an enjoyable job and rewarding as I was to bring new ideas and create themes to coincide with traditional holidays from different faiths around the world.

Before long, a new position in the company was created for me as a senior cook. I was to oversee the food health and safety records of eight of the company's nurseries around the M25 area, making sure they were correct for environmental health inspections. I was also a mentor for the other cooks, their 'go-to person' to help with alternative dietary requirements and ideas for their menus.

Ken often called me during the day and occasionally, I'd prepare lots of great finger food and snacks on my break. He would pick me up from work, and we'd go pick up the kids from school and have a picnic in the park for dinner. Oh, those were certainly the best of times.

The kids had some really cool friends, and they were quite popular. I took pleasure in doing themed birthday parties, where I would do everything from handmade invitations to party bag fillers, party games and homemade party food, all in the chosen theme. Their cakes were always personally made, not shop cakes. There was a Mickey Mouse cake, a magic hat with a rabbit at the top and sparkling candles, a sports car, and a teddy bear cake for the teddy bears' picnic party, where all the guests brought along their favourite teddies. Those were a few to remember. The kids always had the best parties, and their whole class was always invited as they didn't want to upset anyone by leaving them out. They were so considerate at such a young age and were not mean to anyone.

Ken got promoted, and after going for a degree and graduating, he was promoted again. With his income, I really didn't have to work, but it made us live well. Ken's salary covered the mortgage and bills and mine did the shopping and all the other things: school dinner money, trips, haircuts, clothes, shoes and so on.

Our hours increased a little at work, and school term holidays were a struggle. Ken had an Asian friend called Ari from cricket who had recently arrived from India with his wife, and we agreed that they would stay in our home. Tandreema, Ari's wife, became our au pair, so I was able to do longer hours. I also worked as a silver service waitress and a commis chef for an events company that catered to V.I.P.s, the royal family and celebrities. I worked as needed and when there were events, so not every night or weekend—maybe three nights a week and every other Saturday—as I still wanted time for the kids. Plus, being busy kept my mind off the baby I'd lost, which still bothered my mind. Sometimes, a stiff drink cleared and numbed my mind.

There were always spectacular decorations at those events. Funnily enough, it was my dad who'd introduced me and encouraged me to sign up with them, as the head butler of the company and he had become good friends. They catered quite a few dinner parties for the 9th Duke of Wellington, Arthur Wellesley, at Apsley House, where my dad was head of security. Dad always brought home the leftover flower arrangements they gave away at the end of the evening. They were so elaborate. I also had the privilege of doing the same at some functions. I loved the flower arrangements.

There were many grand affairs, such as state dinners at the Guild Hall for heads of state hosted by the Queen and Captain Mark Philips, cocktail parties for Princess Diana at the National History Museum and cocktail parties hosted by Prince Charles and Princess Anne at St James Palace. There were also fancy dinners hosted by Princess Margaret at Blenheim Palace and Hampton

Court Palace, parties for album launches, the cast of the TV series *Eastenders*, Jewish bar mitzvahs and weddings of the elite. I saw them all, and it was amazing until pain started to cripple my arms, it became too hard to carry the amount of covers expected in silver service, and my arms grew too weak to lift. After a good few years of service, I had no choice but to throw in the towel. It was hard as I enjoyed being around our clients and their guests, but that's life, I guess.

My work hours were cut at the nursery as I walked funny if I was on my feet too long, and my hands would freeze in pain if I cut or chopped for too long. It got worse, and after tests were done, I was diagnosed with fibromyalgia. It was crippling, but it was manageable to a certain degree with anti-inflammatory meds.

Summer holidays, Rishon and Ethan had a joint *Action Man* birthday party. Their birthdays were close to each other, and with us having one less income and reduced hours, it made sense to have just one party. Rishon was turning seven and Ethan five. They both loved the same stuff, so it was easy.

Nadia seemed quiet, and I wondered if she was feeling a little jealous, but every time I asked what was wrong she just replied, 'I got a headache,' and she sat quietly with her dolls whilst the boys played outside.

My brother Teddy's girlfriend, Sam, had given birth to a son, and she had just come out of hospital, so I decided to take a train ride with the kids to visit them. Ken was working until late, and Tandreema had the day off. It was a nice summer's day for some mummy and children time.

The train ride was enjoyable but a little long, being as Teddy lived in South East London and we lived North West. The baby was so cute and looked a lot like Rishon. It was nice having another boy in the family. Tthe boys were finally coming to catch up with the many girls. The children played in the garden, and a little while after, Nadia came in as she was tired. The rest dribbled in, and then they decided to play some cards; nothing beats a good game of snap. They were all in a fit of giggles. Then, out of the blue, Nadia threw up on the floor, and everyone froze. I didn't know what to do first. What I really wanted to do was run as I had a phobia about vomiting. Ken was the one who dealt with the kids being sick, but Ken was not there!

Teddy's girlfriend was so good and helped me clean up the floor, and Nadia, whose eyes were red, complained that her tummy and head hurt. It seemed like the beginning of a dreaded stomach bug. The boys grew very quiet and seemed concerned as they really did love each other and didn't like it when one of them was unwell or told off.

After a couple of hours of making sure Nads was okay to journey home, we got ready to leave. Nadia slept for most of the train journey, and Ken picked us up from the train station. It was late, and the kids went straight to bed. In the morning, Nadia was looking normal, with no sign that she had been sick the night before, and the boys were also fine. I had a couple more days at home and then would go back to work.

I got a call from Tandreema the day after returning to work that Nadia had been sick and was complaining of a headache. I called my GP for an evening appointment and left to go home early. I called Ken at work as I started to have a bad feeling about it.

When I got home, Nadia wasn't herself at all. She was lying still in a dark room. The doctor examined her and asked a few questions regarding our family's health background. Given that I was a migraine sufferer, it was diagnosed that she, too, had migraines as it was hereditary. He prescribed some medicine and advised her to keep clear of certain foods such as cheese and chocolate for a while to see if that helped her.

Nadia was sick again the next day, and I wasn't convinced it was migraine, but another trip to the GP gave us the same diagnosis. I felt uneasy and decided to keep a diary. She was sick again twice over two days. Her eyes seemed to bulge when she threw up, and her head hurt at the same time. After a week, the vomiting stopped, but she looked so weak, bless her.

The kids' summer holidays were kind of on hold whilst Nadia was unwell, but the boys played outside with their scooters and biked with the neighbours' kids, so it wasn't all bad.

Nadia seemed a little better, and Tandereema encouraged me to go back to work, saying that she would look after her, so I did. A week passed, and Nadia was okay, but she started to get a little quiet by the end of the week. It was hot outside, and I told myself it was the sun. She was also sensitive to the light. I was nervous, but I couldn't think of why.

Ken reassured me that the doctors had to be right, as two separate doctors had diagnosed the same thing. I know I'm a worrier, but there was something that didn't sit well with me. Nadia was always tired, her head always hurt, and the whites of her eyes were constantly pink.

It was a Friday. I left early to go to work. Ken was home for a much-deserved day off. Around lunchtime, I was called into the office for a phone call; it was Dr Hargreaves! 'Hi, Mrs Sajor. I have another prescription for your husband to pick up.'

'Huh? What? Sorry, you've lost me. What prescription? I thought we had all of them.'

'Yes, this is the one from this morning.'

I was still puzzled. I said okay and that he would pick it up.

I rang home straight away. Ken answered the phone. 'Ken, what's going on? Dr Hargreaves just called about a prescription.'

There was an awkward silence, then he explained. 'Look, Nads was sick again, and she looked really unwell, so I took her to the doctor's.' My head swirled as Ken spoke. A moment later, and my head seemed to spin like a top. I dropped the phone and fell to the ground, sobbing.

My manager came running into the office. 'My God, Maria—what's happened?'

I screamed. 'SOMETHING BAD IS WRONG WITH MY BABY, AND THEY'RE MISSING IT... SOMETHING'S WRONG, SUSAN,' and I cried and cried.

She got one of the staff members to drive me home, but I asked her to drive me to the doctor's first. I calmed down, took my diary out of my bag and marked down an 'S' next to the date. I looked back over the last few weeks. Staring back at me was a distinct pattern of events. I froze.

At the doctor's, I rushed out of the car and asked the receptionist to please call Dr Hargreaves. They knew us very well and had seen how unwell Nadia had looked that morning. She called her out.

I showed Dr Hargreaves the diary of Nadia's headaches and vomiting. I wasn't going crazy. There was a pattern, and she saw it, too: five days of vomiting in the morning once a day, then six days of vomiting twice a day, then a couple of days with nothing, then it would start again. She took the prescription back and gave me something else.

'Now, Mrs Sajor, listen carefully. Give Nadia this medicine after her meal tonight. If she still vomits tomorrow morning, then it's not a migraine. Take her straight to A & E. They'll be waiting for her as an emergency.'

I was shaking, and tears were streaming down my face as my work colleague, Alyson, drove me home.

The boys were home and, knowing them, they'd be anxious, and Nadia would be scared and poorly, so I had to wipe my face, compose myself and act as normal as possible. I explained to Ken all that the doctor had said, and he held me in his arms and said it was all going to be okay. I closed my eyes and held him tightly back.

That evening was spent as normally as possible, playing with the boys whilst Nadia rested quietly with her dolls on the sofa after taking her medication. The morning came, and with it, our greatest fear: Nadia was sick again. We called the hospital to say we were on our way.

She was admitted straight away and annoyingly, all observations carried out were fine. We couldn't understand it. Ken and I were at our wit's end now, as after showing Ken my diary, he agreed that the pattern I was seeing wasn't in my mind, that something was wrong.

The rest of that Saturday, Nads was fine. She was fine on Sunday, and her obs were also fine. The doctors and nurses all joked that she was a mystery child. After talking to the doctor, he said that a CT scan was booked for the Monday, and there was no harm in still getting it done. We could then see about going home, that maybe it really had been a case of bad migraines. In my mind, there was no way.

Just after breakfast on Monday morning, Nads was sick again. Part of me was glad, only because she'd been so well in hospital, and I needed them to see her sick.

She went for the scan in the afternoon, but the medical staff didn't find any signs that anything was majorly wrong, so Ken left to take the boys home for lunch, and I told him I'd call him to pick us up later as I was sure we were going home regardless.

About 20 minutes passed, and three doctors came by Nadia's bed. 'Mrs Sajor? Hello, I'm Dr Parker, the registrar, and these are Drs Reynalds and Simmons, specialists in neurology.' All of that sounded foreign to me.

'Where is your husband? We would like to speak to you both.'

I searched his face as my stomach turned, and I barely got out my words. 'He's gone home to get the boys some lunch.'

'Can you call him back straight away, please? We've found something.'

My heart pounded like a bass drum. I swallowed hard and looked at all their faces, trying to read each one. 'Yes, I will call him, but I need you to tell me straight away as I can't wait. I cannot stand not knowing a moment longer. Please, tell me what is wrong.'

They led me into a room and told me to take a seat as they closed in the door. I felt like I was in a TV documentary; it was so surreal.

Dr Parker allowed Dr Simmons to begin. He took out a pad and began to draw what looked like a Walls sausage and another long shape a little thinner than a pencil. He began to explain: 'There are ventricles in the brain that carry a fluid called cerebrospinal fluid. Your daughter's ventricle is the size of this,' he pointed to the large Walls sausage shape, 'but they should be smaller than this one.' He pointed to the thinner one. 'It's blocked somewhere at the base of her skull. It's a term called hydrocephalus, fluid on the brain. It's common with babies born with spina bifida. She's eight years old now, so that's highly unlikely. Has she knocked her head?'

I was in a daze. I answered, 'No, not that I know of. She just started having lots of headaches and vomiting, and it was put down to migraines until I noticed a pattern. I've kept a diary.'

'We've couriered her scan down to Great Ormond Street Hospital as we haven't got the equipment to look at it in detail for a tumour. Do you know what a tumour is, Mrs Sajor? As she hasn't knocked her head, that could be what's blocking the fluid.'

It was all too much for me. Where was Ken? The nurses had called him, and he was on his way back, but it had felt like hours.

Dr Parker informed me that they were organising an ambulance to take Nadia to Great Ormond Street, which is in central London. I went back to Nadia's bed and watched her play with her toys. She looked so normal. Nothing had shown on her obs, temperature and blood pressure were in the correct rage. We were facing a secret killer.

Ken arrived, and the boys went to the play area. The doctors repeated all they had told me, and Ken slumped into a chair. He fell apart and cried ever so deeply. I held him in my arms and gently whispered, 'Come on, darling. The kids need us. Shhhhh. We gotta keep it together so we don't scare them. It's going to be okay. Specialists finally know now.'

With that, after a few minutes, Ken composed himself. He excused himself to wash his face. I couldn't cry. I needed to be of sound mind and understand everything the doctors had told us.

Work. I had to call work. Only that morning, I'd rung to say she was going for a scan, but we'd more than likely be home that day, and I should be back at work tomorrow.

My manager, Susan, answered the phone. I began strong: 'Hiya. Ummmm… we're not coming out. They found something. We're being transferred to Great Ormond Street Hospital. They're looking for a tumour in her brain. There is fluid blocked.' As the words came out, my voice began to shake, and I broke down. I heard Susan's voice but her words did not register. My world was in a glass bottle, with deep cracks appearing out of nowhere, and it was all about to shatter.

SEASONS

Spring
A word with different meanings
The breaking of a new season
Water glistening in the sun
A child bouncing a toy
Filled with joy, having fun
For me, it was a time of revelation
Stepping out in faith with no hesitation
Moving from flat to house
Making our house into a home
Love fills the atmosphere
Which had lately seemed so rare
Losing our baby had brought us near
I dance when we kiss
I touch the moonlit sky in the night
When my body touches his
His touch, I don't resist
But darkness is still in my mind
Intimacy, for me, is hard to find
Memories still fire back, and the attack is unkind
But what is this?
There is something quite amiss
She is much too small to befall such an illness
It took too long to diagnose
Now there is a crisis
Registrar's words take long to process
And thinking of my child's pain

Makes the word 'tumour' hard to digest
No, this couldn't be
Bad things like this don't happen in our family
Arrrrggghhhh
Okay
Stop
Breathe
It is not confirmed
They are still doing tests, they say
So do what you see the world do
Silence your panic
Pray

Chapter 17

HOW DO YOU SAY GOODBYE?

The consultant met with us straight after we reached GOSH (Great Ormond Street Hospital) and gave us directions to see the optician. He told us it was important to check Nadia's eyes. Everything was moving so fast.

The optician was rather annoyed, and her outburst made us even more anxious. 'How could this go unnoticed? How could your GP not see this?' The vessels behind Nadia's eyes were dangerously swollen and apparently, with this condition, could cause irreversible blindness. Each minute that passed seemed to come with another bombshell. From a low-key day of supposed migraines and vomiting to the full explosion of a life-threatening condition—it was too much.

Back at her bedside, the consultant came in to see Ken and me; the children were with the play assistant. 'Well, Mr and Mrs Sajor, I'm sure, by now, you realise we are dealing with a very sick little girl here. I am so very sorry it has taken so long to detect, but as you can see, it is a very difficult condition to diagnose without the use of a scan. Going forward, we'll need to operate as soon as possible, and there are two options for you to choose.'

For us to choose? I wasn't sure Ken was in any state to make an informed decision. He was so devastated and teared up every time we spoke to a health professional.

The consultant continued, 'They both come with risks. One is that we place a ventriculoperitoneal (VP) shunt in her brain and run a tube to her abdomen, where the excess fluid would be absorbed by her body. The problem was that it would be lifelong, and it may get infected and break periodically, causing her ventricles to collapse or a brain haemorrhage. There was also the possibility for the symptoms of hydrocephalus to return.

'The other is to perform a Ventriculoscope putting a hole in the third ventricle. The risks are in surgery, where the procedure can cause memory loss, problems with speech, balance and vision or a bleed in the brain. It can also cause death. On the positive side, if it is successful, she will need no further treatment, unlike the shunt.

'Do you understand? Which one do you want us to perform?'

'What do you mean?' I shot up out of my chair. 'Surely, you can't put that on us. One is risking her life after the operation, and it's lifelong, and the other is risking her life during the operation, yet no further problems. I can't! I CAN'T CHOOSE.

'What would you do as a professional? You have performed this procedure before. If this were your child, which would you choose?'

There was a silence, and then he sighed. 'If it was my choice, I would choose the Ventriculoscope.'

I felt myself hold my breath and looked at Ken. 'So be it, then. Do that.'

Ken sat in thick, solid silence, and fresh tears fell down his face. All I could do was to hold him in my arms whilst he rested his head on my chest.

The operation was scheduled for the next day. A paediatric nurse came to explain to Nadia that the water in her brain had a blocked lane, and they had to find a way to drain it out by making another little hole to make her better. She understood and wasn't scared in the slightest. The nurse also explained about the needle that would be used to administer the magic liquid that would put her into a deep sleep like Sleeping Beauty. To do this operation, she would have a quarter of her hair shaved off at the front of her head but was assured that her hair would grow back.

My goodness—what was really happening? How could this be happening?

The surgical team came and got Nadia around 11 in the morning, and Ken and I walked alongside her bed as she was wheeled to theatre. She was such a good girl, and nothing phased her. She was prepped, and we were allowed to give her hugs and kisses.

The anaesthetist began to inject the anaesthetic and told Nadia to count backwards from ten. Nadia reached seven, and she was gone. That was when the tables turned. I broke down and sobbed, and Ken held me up with all his strength.

It was four long hours, and in that time, we paced, we sat, we went for a walk, we ate a little but truly had no appetite. I was so scared watching Nadia slip under the anaesthetic. It was like watching her slip away from our lives. Knowing something could go terribly wrong during the operation, including death, was haunting.

The relief of hearing that all had gone well when the surgeon came out filled us with jubilation. There was also no tumour. It will always be a mystery why Nads got this condition. She was probably born with it, and it remained undetected due to it not being a problem. Who knows? She was in recovery and would be out shortly. Ken and I breathed a sigh of relief.

Nads stayed in hospital for a further two weeks and befriended a girl called Melisa, who was 13 years old. She was in to change her shunt and had some other complications with her heart. Melisa lived in Southend near the coast, and her parents decided to leave one evening to go to refresh themselves, change their clothes and collect some things for Mel. They left about six in the evening and were planning to come back in the morning. Melisa was a little rude to her parents and snappy before they left, but they seemed to overlook her tantrums; she was an only child and very sick. Ken and I got to chatting with her parents, and they were a lovely couple.

A little over an hour after they left, Melisa was uncomfortable and wanted her bed adjusted. The play assistant came in and tried to operate the bed, but it was jammed. After another pull and the bed jolted, and Melisa cried out that something hurt in her chest. The play assistant was apologetic, but Melisa burst into tears and wouldn't stop. We called for the nurse, and, before you knew it, there was a big commotion around her bed. A portable X-ray machine was bought in, and all the patients and parents were asked to leave the ward and wait in the playroom.

You could hear Melisa scream in pain and cry, 'It hurts… it hurts,' then there was silence, an eerie silence. I peeped around the door, and the curtain was still around Melisa's bed. The play assistant was tearful as she felt guilty.

After a while, the ward nurse asked the parents to come with her to the next room. She turned to us and said, 'I'm awfully sorry you have been put out of the ward. We will get you back in as soon as possible. We've just lost Melisa.'

I think all the parents gasped in shock. We'd just heard her screaming and crying. How could she be dead? It was most upsetting, and it was agreed that a specialist nurse would break the news to the children.

Melisa's bed was opposite Nadia's, and they had played well together. I couldn't stop thinking of Melisa's poor parents: they hadn't reached Southend yet and could not be contacted. As soon as they arrived home, they would have to turn and come right back to such unthinkable bad news. To think their last conversation had been their daughter shouting at them to go away. Tears hit my eyes.

Melisa's parents broke down and were quite distraught when they came to see us after seeing the medical team. They hugged the play assistant and reassured her it wasn't her fault and not to carry any guilt. They said Melisa had complications, and her shunt had broken, and there was nothing they could do. At that point, after seeing a little girl of 13 die, I was relieved we'd opted for the Venriloscope. The parents hugged and comforted their children, and I thought to myself that it was not good to say goodbye in anger or say mean things as you might never see that person again to say, 'I'm sorry; I love you.'

It was a very emotional couple of days, but then it was time for Nadia to leave. The boys had really missed her and were very excited at her coming home. We all were.

Our little girl was safe and out of the woods. After a couple of weeks, I was ready to go back to work and Nadia to school. Her hair had started to grow back, and it didn't look too bad as it shaded her scalp.

Susan and the staff team welcomed me back. All were relieved at Nadia's recovery. It was coming up to payday, and I couldn't wait. Staying at GOSH had proven quite expensive, with Ken's train fares, petrol and parking metre money and lunches and dinners over the weeks obviously not being a part of our budget.

A couple of days before the end of the month, Susan asked to see me. 'Hey, Maria, how are you settling in?'

I was still quite drained from the ordeal but was getting on in my job. 'I'm fine, thanks. Pacing myself, but it's good to be back.'

'Look, I'm sorry to have to tell you, but you weren't given sick pay.'

I was dumbfounded. 'But Susan, you said to take as much time off to be with Nadia and that you would have me covered. I don't understand what's going on.'

Susan looked down; she couldn't look me in the face. Apparently, because Nadia hadn't died, I was not eligible for compassionate pay. I stopped listening. All I could hear was my own thoughts. What about the bills and responsibilities?

I left the office without another word, and when I arrived home in a panic, I applied for an overdraft, which, thankfully, I got, but it slowly became a noose around our necks.

OUR FATHER WHO ART IN HEAVEN

If someone told me years ago
That my heart would break
That it would shatter in a moment
I'd tell them no
Never would I understand how life could change in just one day
As I sat and listened to what the doctors had to say
Asking me to choose and step in blindly through an open door
Shaking my head, I answered, 'No way. It can't be so…
The direction to retaining life I do not know'
My husband looks towards the floor
Unresponsive, too weak to face this fight

Day is so dark it is like a continuous night
If there are angels
I asked them to come
Sit with my daughter
And make a harmonious sound
Protecting her life
As she goes under the surgeon's knife

There is a sunrise
The sun breaks in with light
And diminishes the voice of doubtful lies
There really are angels
They walk with no wings
The doctors, nurses and surgeons

Family and friends who came to support
And made the time in hospital feel short

I learnt a valuable lesson
That even in your greatest distress
Be kind, be humble
For you never know if you'll see someone another day
Either you or they may pass away
Looking back, when someone asks, 'What last words did they say?'
Let it not be words of hurt and pain
For the memory will drive you insane
It cannot be retracted
The tears will overflow
Never to see your loved one again
So, yes, a valuable lesson learnt
One that was hard to digest
In the midst of all that had transpired
Our mental capacity was truly tired

Dawn has broken on a brand new day
There is a God
This, I know
My mother never took me to church
But with my friends, I'd go
My children have been christened
So Nadia was protected
For I have always followed what the vows directed
To bring them up to know the Lord

This experience brought back those words
I am truly grateful for my daughter's life
Over the years, I have neglected God
I am thankful
And it's time to make things right
I hope God sees me recite 'Our Father, who art in heaven'
And keep my children in His sight

Chapter 18

A WALK TO REVELATION

Nadia continued to get better, but our financial responsibilities gradually got worse. Yes, I worked, but the pain in my joints was unbearable. My duties and salary had already been cut short due to the fibromyalgia, but what could I do? I couldn't stop, and we couldn't afford to stop. The pain advanced from my arms, hands and hips down to my legs, the soles of my feet and my lower back. The doctor said it was stress-related, which made sense because I was definitely stressed.

There were mornings I had difficulty getting out of bed. Stepping out of bed made me drop to the floor, as I couldn't stand because my feet were exceptionally painful. What was really happening? This was something I often asked myself.

Ken started to get a bit snappy. I sensed that an old demon was coming back, and I felt myself walking on eggshells just to keep the peace, but it didn't stop arguments from breaking through. The silent treatment bothered me. If I did something, then he should at least say what it was, but the more he stayed quiet about what had him so disgruntled, the more he grunted good morning or goodnight, the more frustrated I got until it was too much, and I popped. Our arguments started to be more frequent. This from the man of my dreams, who had made my knees weak for months after I'd met him. His eyes had lost their sparkle. Maybe it was because he hardly smiled unless he was with his friends, and even then. His eyes remained dry. His absent tears made me feel his heart turned cold and hard. Maybe it was because his heart was also becoming dry.

Our shouting turned into physical bouts, where I threw a punch in rage, and he shoved and slapped me back, to which I retaliated, trying to hit him back. I say try, as he would then use all his strength to restrain me. We stopped when we came to our senses after hearing one of the children start crying.

What had become of us? Financial hardship always seemed to put Ken in a deep, sombre mood, which affected our relationship.

I remember when we first moved into our short-term accommodation. We were not financially well off, but we loved on each other through it all. I guess it was the added pressures of the additions to the family additions, my maternity leaves, my cut pay, my cut hours, our mortgage, my car, his car… Yes, our dynamics had changed considerably, but didn't everyone's? Surely, every couple didn't fight like us.

It got so bad one day that Ken reached for my favourite bomber jacket and cut it up with a knife, shouting it was his money that had bought my clothes, so he could do what he wanted to them. I watched in rage but dared not tackle him with a knife in his hands. I honestly can't remember what sparked that argument. I cried and cried. I cried for my jacket, for the situation, for the hurt, for my marriage. I cried for Ken as he had changed. Something was bothering him. Something was up, but we still loved each other, right?

Who could I go to? There was no one. There was no way I could let Mum know. Or Cam. Let them know my marriage was crumbling? Not in this lifetime. Not so they could laugh at me!

Tell Bernel? I'd already told her some things but not the full extent. Tell her so she could cuss me out for still staying in it?

Tell Ken's sister? She might tell off Ken, then he'd know I'd spoken to people about our marriage, and hell would break loose.

No, something told me the only trusted ear I could tell it all to was God Himself.

I started attending the Church of England church at the bottom of our road. It just so happened to be the same church I'd gone to for Sunday School as a child, where my sister, brother and Ken and I all got married and where Nadia had been christened. The church had a sentimental history, and I needed to feel love, to feel normal. Growing up, I'd always heard that God loved all His children. I was His child, too, and I needed to feel His love—any love. Ken had promised. He'd vowed to love me till death do us part. I thought that meant physical death, not the death of our marriage! I thought my old memories of fake, adulterated love had been buried, but the rejection I felt creeping in was like resurrecting those dry old bones.

On Sundays, I found peace in the rituals of the service, and I felt good doing my part in taking the children and sending them to Sunday School as I had committed to doing when Nadia was in hospital. I also struck up a good conversation with the vicar and over time, I knew I had a confidant in her, and I started telling her about my married life.

That was Sunday morning taken care of. There was always tea, coffee and biscuits after service, and I always stayed behind to chat, stalling going back home. Once home, I dove into cooking a typical Trinidadian Sunday dinner. Come rain or shine, I made sure we had the ingredients to do that. Sunday wouldn't be Sunday without rice 'n' peas, macaroni pie, brown stew chicken, crab 'n' calalloo, plantains, sweet potatoes and salad. A tall glass of wine always accompanied me as I cooked. Cooking was like therapy for me, and the wine helped block the tension in the house.

During the week, I needed a nightly shot of straight rum to block out Ken and numb the rejection I felt when he came home from work, so my sanity stayed intact, and I was able to function.

Unfortunately, there was still bickering under our breaths, and we both adopted a provoking spirit. There were times when, out of the blue, we would have a good day that led to great days. Those were the days after we'd made love, and he'd whisper how sorry he was and that he loved me and wanted me, that he needed me, that he was just under stress at work. There were things going on with the management, but he couldn't—more like wouldn't—tell me what it was. Being intimate took down his stress levels and made him a nicer person. When I knew that was where the evening was heading, I took another (largeish) shot of rum so I could keep the memories of the past at bay. I had awoken the demons from the closet of my soul, and every time we were intimate, the flashbacks confused me as to what was real and what was in my imagination. I spent most of the time love-making battling my mind to stay focused on that it was indeed Ken making love to me and not one of the dark men of my past.

Ken's temperament moved like waves. I was grateful when it peaked, but the peak meant the only way after was down!

One day, I went to pick up the children from school and across the playground, Ken walked towards us, which was a nice surprise. By the time he got to us, I saw he was forcing a smile as he said hello. I tried to search his face but could not read it. Something wasn't quite right, though.

He leaned over to whisper in my ear, 'Babes, look—let's take the kids to the park to blow off some steam. We need to talk.'

I tried not to sound bothered. 'Yeah, sure. Why not?

'Kids, come on. Let's head to the park before we go home. If you're really lucky, you can get an ice lolly if the ice cream man is there.' I couldn't help but smile at their excitement as they ran to the car.

As Ken and I got to the car, my mind was working overtime. What could it be? I didn't dare ask. I patiently waited.

They couldn't get out of the car fast enough, running to the slide and swings. Ken and I walked to a bench where we could keep a watchful eye on them. 'Look, I'm not going to lie. There have been some problems at work... I've been laid off.'

I stared at him blankly, trying to slow down my thinking. 'For how long? Laid off. What does that mean?'

'Maria, let go. Sacked.' He bowed his head into his hands and gave the biggest sigh. I'd never known Ken not to have a job.

'What's going to happen? The mortgage, the bills. I don't earn enough, Ken. I'm scared.'

Ken hung his head as he continued, 'The end of the month is my last pay. I got to job hunt. I'll try a different borough. Something will come up. Until then, it's going to get a hell of a lot rougher. Like I said, my last pay is the end of this month.'

Silence. Just the children's laughter in the background and the traffic hustling by. I had promised the children ice lollies but felt it would be like spending a hundred pounds! It was just ice lollies, for Christ's sake; it wasn't going to break the bank.

Fear and panic were setting in, but I hung onto Ken's words. He'd job hunt and would have a job in no time. He was skilled, he was qualified, he had his degree, and he was good at what he did. How hard could it be?

I enjoyed the children's happy faces at their choices of ice lollies; they were my constant joy.

It was going on six months, and Ken had gotten no further than a second interview with the few he had. Companies inviting him for interviews were initially interested in him, but as soon as they received his references, it was all over. The more knockbacks he got, the bitterer and madder he got. Ken was constantly in a bad mood. He even got a little snappy with the children, and when I pulled him up on it, he quarrelled that I was undermining him. I unlocked the scratched vinyl in my mind that used to play the words, 'Shut up,' and I played it again now. I obeyed. For peace of mind, I shut up, not just my mouth, but everything within me.

It was another four attempts before Ken finally got a position. It was not quite what he wanted—fewer hours and less pay—but it was a job. There was a lot of catching up to do as we were so behind in our mortgage payments that letters had started to come in threatening repossession due to a string of broken payment promises.

Water rates, gas, electric bills, catalogue payments—everything was behind in payments. I did what I could, but I was still living in the overdraft. A part of me felt guilty. Bottled up with my dislike of the man I'd loved so much was the guilt of having babies, staying out of work to be a mother in their early years and with Nadia in GOSH for the entire time she was there, but what else could I have done? My children needed me. Nadia had literally been on her death bed, had nearly gone blind… Yes, I'd nearly lost my mind by taking out an emergency overdraft, but it had been done, and there we were.

Cam encouraged us to go to a party for a longtime friend of ours who was turning 40. Ken wasn't keen, but Cam wouldn't take no for an answer. I was glad she talked him round, as I needed a night out to dance off the stress. It was summer, and the days were quite warm, but the nights were quite chilly, so I was excited to think about what to wear. It was just a few days away, and I made sure to take double shots of rum at night to ignore and block out any negative vibes and get me to sleep quickly.

It was a Saturday night, and we dropped the children off to my Mum and Dad's earlier in the day. Whilst we got ready, Ken played some music and, thankfully, was in a relatively good mood. I fixed myself a drink so I could stay in mine.

The party was packed when we got there. The living room was a through-lounge, and there was hardly any room in there, with these big, double speaker boxes on either side of the room. Past the kitchen was the door to the garden, where many were liming as they smoked. I looked around, but there was no sign of Cam yet. Great.

Ken and I ended up in the living room where the main party was and said hi to the few faces we knew. After a while, Ken said he was going for a smoke and that he'd be back. He took ages. I was just about to squeeze past people to go meet him when I saw that Cam had finally turned up with Patrick. She stayed in the room with me, and Pat went out to meet Ken for a smoke and lime outside, too. They were playing some good music, and we danced freely. Then, the DJ spun some lovers rock, and I felt this hand out of nowhere touch my elbow to pull me to dance. I turned and said that my husband was outside. He smiled and replied, 'Well, I better keep his wife dancing then so she doesn't get lonely.'

Cam giggled and turned away, nudging me to go ahead. It was not like I was having an affair. It was just a dance, and I loved dancing. Ken had left me for well over an hour, so what did he expect? So, yes, I danced with that guy, who was a friend of a friend, and anyway, he knew my sister, so it felt safe and above board. We danced twice, and he pulled me for a third. I kept looking towards the door, silently praying that Ken would come and save me as I didn't like the way the guy was getting comfortable with me.

Before long, I felt a tap on my shoulder. I turned; it was Ken. I smiled, thankful to see him, but he didn't smile back. He just said that we were going.

I frowned. I hadn't danced with Ken yet as he'd spent most of the night—well, all of the night—outside, so I was a tad vexed.

We said our goodbyes, and Ken went to the car to wait for me as I saw some people I knew, so my goodbyes stretched out a little longer. By the time I got to the car, Ken was mumbling under his breath.

'Ken, what's up with you? You didn't have to leave like that.'

'Yeah, and you didn't have to be all over some man like that either.' Oh, boy—did my blood under my skin.

'You mean to tell me that you dropped me off at the party and headed outside to smoke and drink with the lads and expected me to stand up all night? I'm sick of you. All you do is moan and groan. You find fault with everything. If nothing goes Ken's way, then all hell breaks loose. YOU GRATE ME, TRYING TO MAKE ME DANCING WITH SOME GUY AN ISSUE. WHERE WERE YOU, HUH? I SHOULD'VE DANCED WITH 10.'

Ken drove like a maniac in anger, like he was trying to be more vexed than me. 'YOU BEHAVED LIKE A SLUT, NO RESPECT FOR ME. HOW DARE YOU BE RUBBING UP ON SOME FRICKIN' MAN THAT YOU DON'T KNOW?'

I was hot, boiling hot, not from heat but from anger. Who the backside did he think he was shouting at and calling degrading names at? Over a flipping dance!

I wanted to punch and kick him. I wanted to scream, and my head felt like it had blown up so much it would explode. Ken was shouting. I was shouting. The car was swerving. It was a crazy scene. Luckily, it was about four in the morning, and the road was clear of cars, BUT there were traffic lights, poles, lamp posts, traffic islands, trees, parked cars and railings... an accident waiting to happen.

I screamed at him to stop the car, but he accelerated. I literally saw my children, family and friends flash before my eyes as the car screeched to a stop when we reached a red light. I flung open the door and got out.

As I slammed the door shut, Ken shouted, 'WALK, BITCH,' and he sped off.

So there I was, alone in the middle of the road. It was dark, and I had heels on and a party dress with a jacket. Great look! Tears stung my eyes, but I welcomed the cold air to cool me down and to get my bearings. Okay, so he'd driven off. Great. I started walking in the direction he'd driven as no doubt he'd stopped farther up the road to wait, or maybe he'd double back when he calmed down. I loved Ken—really, I did—but he sparked such anger in me that it suffocated out the love and replaced it with hate, yet when things were good, the love was there as if it had never left.

I walked for a good five minutes, and there was no sign of his car. The road was coming up to a curve. Maybe he was waiting beyond it. I started to quarrel in my head that he was such a cow to make me walk for so long. He could've at least doubled back. I told myself that when I got back into the car, I wouldn't say a word and keep the silent treatment going until he apologised for being such a dickhead.

I kept walking. I walked to the curve, and as the road straightened, all I saw were street lights, parked cars and the odd car passing by on either side of the road.

He'd left me? Oh, how the tears burnt my eyes. I heard a car slow down from behind and pull up beside me. I turned, expecting to see Ken, but it was two guys in a car asking me if I wanted a ride.

I put on the most confident voice I could muster and told them. 'No, I'm cool, thanks. I'm actually nearly home.'

They smiled and said that if I was sure, then okay. They actually seemed genuinely concerned that I was out on my own, obviously stranded, no matter how much I tried to look as if nothing were wrong.

Just as confidently, I picked up my pace. That was close. They could've been guys with bad intentions. I was dressed inappropriately for that time of the morning, just minutes before five.

It was clear Ken had driven completely off, and I was pissed. Evil, wicked bastard. How could he do that?

I stopped walking. Where was I? Nearly home, my foot! I was far. Surely, he hadn't left me to walk. I was seven to eight miles from home, wearing a short dress, jacket and yes, heels. I dared not take them off as the pavement was literally stone cold and damp. I thought to walk to a police station, to go to the park and rest on a bench, to sit on the cold, wet, moss-covered bench, to walk to a friend's house... and tell them what? The tears burst the banks and streamed down my face. Was I not loved, cared for, valued? How could he have left me?

I wanted to sob, but it was too cold for an over-wet face and bulging eyes. It was half past five. The buses would be running by then. I could take a long bus ride and make him worry. Let him think of an answer when my mum asked where I was.

Arrrrgh—I had no money; I was totally screwed.

I continued to walk, stopping to look expectantly up at passing cars, but he wasn't coming back. I filled my mind with images of the children, flowers, funny moments to mask the thoughts of rejection, indecent touches, Grandad's kiss, boys in the bushes—we'll show you ours, then you show us yours... Had they done that to all girls or singled me out due to the sign I had on my forehead, invisible to all but males, that read, 'Use her. Abuse her,' when performing sexual acts in undignified positions? Yes, all of these images came flooding in.

Good for nothing, useless girl. No one wants you. No one hears you. They refuse to listen. Not even your husband wants you. Look at you. He doesn't care. He left you in the street at four in the morning and look at you, suffering because pride had stopped you from speaking out the truth of your marriage. It's not on the rocks. It's on a precipice!

Flowers. Think flowers: roses, lilies, daffodils, tulips and forget-me-nots...

Forget me not.

Water. Think water. Warm water, remember? He loves you. He used warm water, remember? Remember?

My thoughts were so exhausting I didn't even realise I'd reached my road. I'd walked without thinking of the route. I'd just walked. It was all I could do to take my mind off the throbbing pain in my feet and lower back. I felt crippled.

The mind is a strange, intelligent force. I was home, the sun was up, and it was 6.10 a.m. I'd walked for two hours in heels in the freezing cold.

I opened the door. I saw Ken sitting on the settee. It's not that I was giving him the silent treatment; I just had no words, and I was exhausted. I felt nothing but excruciating pain in my feet, legs and back and had nothing for him. He was obviously up worried about where I was but pride and ignorance had stopped him from coming back. It was all good. I knew what I was worth: just a cup of warm water.

In church the Sunday before, the vicar had mentioned the part in the Bible where Jesus said that lukewarm was neither hot nor cold, so He vomited it out of His mouth. He was speaking of a lukewarm church, but I guess warm water was just the same. Maybe warm water wasn't enough to equal love; I'd measured my worth by something fit to make you vomit.

I headed to the drinks cabinet, took down a water glass, poured it half-full of rum, and it was all gone in three big swigs. It wasn't long before everything zoned out; the pain in my body and mind numbed, and sleep came quickly.

Alison Ryan -Chase

MEDICINAL PURPOSES

I'm wondering what is inside of me
Drying me out, making me thirsty
I pull a glass in the face of calamity
Filling it with living poison
Saving me from insanity
I can imagine a different life
Intoxication breaks free the colours of the rainbow
Straightening the curve balls of confusion
Escaping entrapment of mental delusion

My heart beats so fast
To save it from breaking
It's placed in a cast
Attempting at all costs to make this love last
Yet it seems I fight a losing battle
There are so many cracks between us we've become fragile
His moods have turned him bilingual
Love and hate, both speak fluently
Translated within me so expeditiously

Breathe
Let not anger be your curse
Your daughter had no use for a hearse
She came home healthy
Don't let this trial steal your faith
Fan the flames from lost employment
Don't know what to do for your husband?

You go to church now... Pray!

I'm calling from within, 'Feed me'
I'm thirsty for the liquid that makes me dizzy
It shuts out the noise
Closing the canals of my ears
Blinds me from seeing your tears
My anaesthesia to the quarrelling and pain
Whatever happened to the love back then?
You have hidden from family and friends
The arguments and fights between you and Ken
Do you think it's you they'll blame?
Or worried that you'll tarnish his name
When they realise what's going on and feel shame

You are moving in the right direction
Receiving guidance from a trusted reverend
Attending church on most Sundays
Learning how to live your life
But have you disclosed to the vicar,
Your dependency on liquor?

Something's got to give
Something's got to die so you can live
Walking eight miles towards a turbulent home
Punishment? Ignorance?
Or just plain wickedness?
We need to find another solution
Increasingly filling your gut with pollution

Desperately creating an illusion

There's got to be another way
There is power in the tongue
So watch what you say
Tearing each other down day after day after day
You are both still relatively young
And married life, in hindsight, has only just begun

Chapter 19

WHAT DID YOU DO MARIA?

Ken had settled into his job, but we had not settled back into each other since the night of the party a few weeks before. I was living in disbelief that not only had he left me, but he had left a young woman so far away from home in the wee hours of the morning in party clothes and heels without thinking about her well-being and safety. The more I thought about it, the more upset I got. I just couldn't get over it. That man had promised to love me. He'd made vows. He wasn't supposed to be like other men.

Ken was riddled with guilt, and he used it to be more spiteful and not talk to me, communicating with a vague yes or no in a grunt.

Ken flew into fits of rage sometimes, not necessarily at me, but other random things, mainly debts piling up and debt collectors pressuring us for payments. Mostly, everything was in his name, so he took most of the grief. That's when he started breaking things. The cabinet doors in the kitchen were smashed in, light fittings in the dining room were broken, the wall was chipped in the living room, and there was a broken lamp shade in the corridor. I began to dislike our beautiful home; it was turning ugly. Every room had a sign and reminder of our hurt and anger. The only signs of love were the children.

Ken got into the habit of throwing things. In an argument about taking out the rubbish, he told me to take it out myself. He was being so ignorant for no reason and eventually grabbed up the two rubbish bags and stormed past me out the backdoor, which was made up of glass panels, calling me a stupid bitch. It was a common thing now, cussing me out.

I shouted at him to go to hell, and in that split second, he threw one of the bin bags back at me as I shut the door to guard myself. It banged into the door and shattered two of the panels. I looked at him with disgust, and he looked at me the same way.

He started cursing in the garden, something I detested and felt so embarrassed and ashamed about. It was so hard to face the neighbours after he'd made such a racket. What on earth did the neighbours think? What were they saying?

I would stay inside for days after a huge row. If I had to go to work, then I snuck out early and literally ran to the car so as not to be seen or spoken to.

Ken came charging into the house like a bull, still ranting. It was just a bin, for crying out loud. Why was it such a big deal to put it out on time for the garbage truck?

I turned and screamed at him to shut up and to move his cricket bag from the middle of the corridor. As I stamped up the stairs, he grabbed his bag with his cricket uniform and equipment in it and threw it at me. It hit my back, and I buckled and fell down the stairs.

When I jumped up, I went for his face. We wrestled to the floor, and I just stopped. I'd had enough, and my back was really hurting. I felt deflated, out of breath. 'ENOUGH. ENOUGH, KEN. What are we doing? WHY?'

He rolled off me and just sat there on the floor and began to cry. I wasn't used to seeing him cry at all. I just stared at him. He looked pathetic. My heart was cold towards him, and I was far from moved by his breakdown.

I got up, fixed my clothes, dried my face and walked to the drinks cabinet.

Mum came over a few days later to measure for new curtains. I was quiet, and every so often, I struggled to hold back tears. Should I tell her? Maybe she could help. How many more excuses could I possibly have to explain breakages?

'Maria, how you looking like someone dead? What's up with you? What happen?'

I sat down on my bed and began to tell Mum what happened a few days before with the dustbin and cricket bag. I expected her to be shocked and sympathetic. She listened, and her first question to me was 'What did you do to deserve it?'

What did I DO? Tears stung me, and I'm sure my heart had palpitations. I stopped talking. Yes, it was me; always me, worthless, ugly, fat, childish, deserving of all things bad, deserving of rejection, deserving of wrongful seduction, deserving to be trampled on, slapped and sworn at with degrading words.

What had I done to deserve it, she'd asked. I sucked up the tears, refusing to let one to drop. 'I don't know, Mum. I guess something.'

'Well, Maria, what can I say? Talk to Ken. He is a good man. You make all these children and have the man under pressure to pay the mortgage and other bills. Back off him a bit and allow him to be a man in his own right. Things will get better. All this is part of marriage.'

Wow! No, 'Are you okay? Do you want me and Dad to have a word with him? How's your back? How's your joints?' Nope. Just, 'You made the children by yourself. What did you do to provoke him, to warrant that behaviour towards you?' My goodness.

I couldn't be bothered anymore. I changed the conversation to talk about her approaching trip to Barbados. What was the point of talking about anything else? I should've known better.

I decided not to talk anymore.

I managed to nail a job as a weekend chef in a place called Victoria in London. It was a bit of a trek away, and it meant I could no longer attend church on Sundays. There was a midweek Bible class, and I decided to go to that, at least, but there was no way Ken would take the children to Sunday school, so they had to stop going for a couple of weeks. It wasn't until the parishioners heard why I'd stopped coming that they rallied together and got a few people to pick up the children on Sundays, which was lovely. It got them out of the house, as their dad was no longer fun to be around.

The old VIP events company I'd worked with years before was recruiting, and I thought, why not? If I did three or four nights mid-week and nights after work on Saturday, surely my arms and back could manage that. So that was me: three jobs, seven days a week, plus looking after the house and kids. Now, people might think that's fair, but I hardly saw the children. It was basically 'hi' and 'bye', but it wasn't forever, I guess, and it was a sacrifice I was willing to make to bring more money in and take the 'pressure' off of Ken. It also got me away from Ken, so we weren't in each other's faces, which meant fewer fights.

The numbers had grown at the nursery. Although my hours had been cut and there was less pay, the workload increased, but I had to keep pressing. My head had a heavy feeling, like a dull headache, but I still wanted to go see Mum and Dad off at the airport. They were going to Barbados and Grenada to visit family and attend the wedding of a close family friend.

Camela, Patrick and my brother Curtis were also at the airport. We talked and laughed as we waited for the gate to be called. Suddenly, I had a bad feeling, like a panic attack come over me. I needed sugar, fast; I felt I was going to pass out.

Cam passed me a sugar sachet from her food tray, and I emptied it in my hand and slowly licked it up. I was sluggish and couldn't move fast. I felt one-sided and really slow, like someone had spiked my drink. I didn't want to worry Mum and said that I felt much better, but I felt as if I was losing my mind.

We said our goodbyes, and I told Mum I'd call her and let her know I was fine once I thought they'd landed and settled.

They went through safely. The flight was on time.

I left with Cam and Pat. I slept in the car for the 50-minute drive home. When we arrived, I got out of the car with difficulty but tried my best to look normal. I didn't want them worrying, and I had things to do, such as pick up the children from school. I told Cam I'd call her later and that I most probably hadn't eaten on time. My speech was so slurry, but I guess it was due to the sluggish feeling I had. Pat helped me to the door and inside. I insisted that they shouldn't worry and that I'd be fine and promised them a phone call later that evening.

I had just over a three-hour nap before getting ready to collect Nadia, Rishon and Ethan. The school was just over a mile away. I got into the car. I knew I was not fit to drive, but I had no choice. I couldn't think straight. I got into the car and did one thing at a time, slowly and with deep concentration. The car moved at 20 miles per hour, but it felt like 60! Other car drivers overtook me, but I was at least smart enough to drive with the hazards blinking, so it would seem as if the car was giving the trouble and not me, the driver. Only God knows how I made it to the school.

I saw my friend, Mary, and told her I wasn't well. As a couple of her children were in the same class as mine, I asked if she could bring them out for me.

Thankfully, she did, and after reassuring her I'd be okay, I set off home. The children seemed to know to be quiet as they saw I wasn't quite right. To this day, I don't know how I made it home. There were no other cars on my side of the street like there usually were outside of our house, so I was able to drive straight to a stop without manoeuvring around them.

I gave Nadia the keys to open the front door and told the kids I'd be in shortly. I sat there absolutely shaken. It was as if someone had drugged me. I was there but not there. I could hear but struggled to make sense of what I heard.

I got into the house and literally fell onto the sofa. An hour passed, and Ken arrived home. I asked him to ring my night work and let them know I was sick. I could tell he wanted to strop, but he also saw that I was in no way well enough to take his shit.

I went to bed. I called no one!

In the morning, my speech was still dragging, and I called my GP. After hearing me speak, he asked who was home with me. Ken was still there as he had a very late start. Dr Peterfield asked that he take me straight to the hospital, and he would let them know I was coming. He said he wanted to rule out a mini-stroke as he was concerned, given my symptoms.

I could tell that Ken was more annoyed than concerned, and I hated him for showing it. I told him that he shouldn't bother. 'I'll ask our neighbour a couple doors down to take me.'

He wouldn't hear of it only because he knew how shameful it would look, to be honest. So, he took me.

After seeing consultants, taking blood tests and a CT scan, I was diagnosed with having had a TIA (mini-stroke). After hearing about my ordeal, they were shocked I'd managed to drive and advised that if it happened again, under no circumstances was I allowed to get behind the wheel of a car.

I stayed in a few days for observation. Ken had to take over and manage the house. There was no room for depression or bad moods; the children needed him. I needed him.

I finally got Ken to call Cam and my brothers to let them know what had happened. When they asked about the cause of the stroke, Ken repeated what the doctor had told us. It was due to stress!

Whilst in hospital, I had a few more TIAs, and my speech totally went. I could not form words and sounded like a deaf person. I was unable to find words, which made the sentences I tried to form sound like gibberish.

My vision was blurred, and I also had double vision, the tinnitus was extremely loud in both of my ears, and the noise drove me mad. I also had right-side weakness in both my arm and leg.

I suffered from multiple symptoms, including vertigo, and the doctors had me heavily medicated. I didn't know my life could end up so bad. I was to be 30, and I would meet the new decade disabled by a condition associated with old people. I had dreams and aspirations, and not being an able-bodied person put those at the risk of not transpiring. I was in a dark place.

I was discharged from hospital with physiotherapy to be done as an outpatient and was also to attend speech therapy every week to learn to speak again using Ladybird Books, such as the Peter and Jane series used in kindergarten for first-time readers.

Ken's cousin was a darling. Sammy took me shopping and helped me get to appointments. She didn't live too far away, and she made herself available. I confided in her quite a bit about Ken and my volatile relationship. At last, I had someone who saw and believed me and didn't suggest that I deserved any of it. My speech was really bad, and she was my mouthpiece when in shops, as strangers found it hard to understand me.

I was under outpatient care at Charing Cross Hospital as they have a hyperacute stroke unit. When I attended my appointment for the first time, the neurologist was shocked at the amount of work I had done, plus looking after three young children and said he wasn't surprised that my body had said enough was enough and shut down. He said I had been under too much stress. I asked when I might recover, he replied that the best thing for me to do was to retreat and convalesce away from the children and my present environment if it was possible, and that might speed up my recovery. Other than that, he said the brain was a very complex thing, that even as neurologists, they had much to learn. He couldn't tell me how long I would be like that or if I would make a full recovery. That was I had to go by.

I was indefinitely signed off work from the nursery and had to hand in my notice at my weekend job and at the VIP events catering. We were back on one salary, and Ken had not an ounce of compassion. He was livid that I was sick and refused to drive me to appointments. He said that if I was too sick to work, then he was too sick to work, too, and he stopped going to work full-time. He told them he was sick, went to work part time and stopped paying the mortgage. He sat around the house in a sulk and stopped talking to everyone. Looking back, I can't imagine what was going through the children's minds to have me so sick and their dad off the rails.

Ken started sleeping downstairs. He came up to the bedroom occasionally and slept on the farthest side of the bed, away from me. I was so doped up with drugs that I didn't care. The drugs I had to take were so strong and had me more like a zombie than the actual stroke had.

At first, I used to think I was having erotic nightmares. I felt the sensation of intimacy, but the scenes in my mind made no sense. They were either in bushes or under something like a dining table covered with a cloth, or I was in a car or in a room I didn't recognise. I saw the faces of men. Some I knew, and some were complete strangers. I tossed and turned and woke up in cold sweats, frantic and scared or, sometimes, with a surreal feeling of euphoria, which made no sense as I was far from being happy. Then I realised that my underwear was twisted or not there.

I felt haunted and troubled by a dark spirit. No, there was nothing ghostly about any of it. It was simply my husband taking advantage of my medication, waiting for me to be deep in sleep before he had his way with me. I was not in my right mind, and I couldn't fight him off. I craved being touched and loved, but we both knew had I been in my right state of mind, there was no way I would have allowed him to come near me.

When I realised what was happening, I tried to argue with Ken, but the more I got upset, the more my speech collapsed into a mess, and when it did, Ken took the piss, mimicked my speech in my face and walked away. Even in sickness, I was abused and treated as if I had no value. I needed to get away.

My brothers and Cam put together and paid for a ticket for me to go to Trinidad to stay with family. Cam and Teddy finally saw what I'd been going through, and they were worried that I would get so stressed that I'd have a full-blown stroke. Sammy worked for an airline and got discounted tickets and booked to come with me; I had given Sammy my passport as I didn't think it would be safe in my house.

It was May and going on five months since I'd had the strokes. The weather was quite warm. I had been taking little walks by myself, just to local shops. I worked on my speech, and was understandable if I spoke shortly and slowly.

One day, I took a walk to the local pharmacy. I had to go to the same shops all the time as I suffered from short-term memory loss. I also forgot how to cook. Yes, me, a chef, forgot how to cook—I couldn't put a salad together, and I couldn't boil rice. An aunt used to cook and bring enough to last two days. Slowly, people were seeing what Ken was doing to me and to our little family, and many were mad at him, which in turn made the things he did more horrible.

I went to the pharmacy and, as I was at the counter, I turned to see a very dear old friend I'd grown up with. He had come to my wedding and, over the years, I would bump into him as he was on the local high street, giving out leaflets and inviting people to his church and church concerts; I remembered there were rumours that a group of the guys on our old road had 'found Jesus'.

I hadn't seen Winston since I'd got sick, and he would have freaked out if he heard me. I needed to get past him without him seeing me, but he was right there by the front door, and he was in a deep conversation with no intention of moving soon. I had to just try to walk past fast with a quick acknowledgement. As soon as I approached, his conversation ended. What timing! There was nowhere to run or hide. He saw me and broke out in a huge smile, so happy he was to see me.

'Hey, Maria. What's happening, man? Long time.'

I smiled, scared to open my mouth, not sure of how he would react.

He looked at me and said, 'What's up?'

I took a deep breath in and said, 'Don't be alarmed,' and his face dropped, and his eyes bulged in disbelief at what he'd just heard.

'Naaaa... What happened? What's wrong with you? How long you've been like this? Maria, what happened?'

I put my hands up for him to stop. 'Listen carefully; don't be scared. It's still me inside. I had a few mini-strokes, and my speech went, but it's much better now.'

He looked baffled. 'What? THIS is much better?'

I told him as much as I could, but I couldn't talk long as my speech always declined when I became fatigued.

'I've heard enough. Maria, look—you've tried doctors, specialists, physiotherapists, neurologists, and you are still like this since January? Do me a favour: try Jesus! What have you got to lose? We got a revival service on starting tomorrow, and I'm telling you: your life will change, and you will get your healing. Just promise me you will come. Will you come?'

What really did I have to lose? What harm could it be?

I nodded. I'd burnt myself out by talking. I asked Winston to please drive me home as I was scared I'd get lost as I was forgetting my bearings; he did.

As he drove, he spoke highly of his church and made it sound so exciting. He wrote down simple directions. It was just one bus, and the bus stopped right outside the church.

As he helped me out of the car and to my door, he asked me again, 'You sure you will come? I want God to touch you.'

I smiled and nodded, too exhausted to talk. He seemed to understand because he said goodbye, and I waved.

Tomorrow, I would go to church.

Alison Ryan -Chase

IT CAN'T BE...

No way
It can't be
Is that the same guy you met at Panama?
The one you said turned heads
Who made your heart stop as if you were dead?
No way
It can't be
Is it that same guy you danced with all night
Conversed with until he took you to a natural high?
No way, Maria
It can't be
You mean to say that's the same guy who made you weak at the knees
Who showed you what it meant to be loved
Who took the stain away of the dirty touch
Unlocked the chains and set you free
The same guy who made vows to you
Dedicated his love when he said, 'I do'?
Him?
He's the one
Who is relentless in abusing you?

Oh, my gosh
I never would have known
Men seem to be the same
Whether young or old
Who can be trusted with your spirit and soul?

Not to break your body under the false illusion of being whole
Tit-for-tat developed into the hills of a mole
Built into mountain tops before your eyes
And daily, everything within you cries.
Longing for…
Seeking
Deserving a love
That will materialise
But everything turned out to be lies
There was no natural high
It was a mirage
Infatuation awaiting sabotage
A coalition with love and strife
How is it possible to destroy the hopes of one's wife?
Is this seriously all I must expect from life?

My friend now tells me there is hope
He says there is One who cares
And invites me to come along to hear
How His kind of love redeems and repairs
Heals your body, soul and mind
He rants with excitement that He is one-of-a-kind
And to be real, He is the most genuine love I'll ever find.

So, yes, I'll go
You never know
Something needs to go
To die…
And be reborn

Is that possible,
To heal me from the symptoms of a stroke?
Winston, this better not be one of life's jokes
I've run out of laughter
I've run out of steam
I've run out, I'm clean out
I shout out…
SEE ME!
If You, God, are there
If You can hear
Restore my body
These burdens are not fair
I'm putting the last of me in Your hands
Help me to rise up, to stand
No way
It can't be
Am I really going to find the only love me?

Chapter 20

GIFTS OF A REVIVAL

It was a bright Sunday morning. I wasn't sure what to expect that day, but I did want to explore. I was intrigued by what Winston had said, and it somehow stayed in my head, even the directions. Normally, I forgot the things I did in the morning by the evening, and I especially forgot what I did the day before. Maybe it was a sign.

I let the children go to their normal Sunday School and got ready to go to Winston's church.

He was right: it was a relatively easy journey. I got there about ten minutes early and there were a lot of young people greeting each other and talking and children running around. I took a seat towards the back as I didn't see Winston and waited patiently. A young lady came up to me after a few minutes to say hello, something I dreaded as I didn't want anyone to talk to me as it meant I would have to speak back, and I was self-conscious about my speech. 'Hello, my name is Lisa. Nice to meet you. Is it your first time here?'

I looked at her and smiled, anxious about opening my mouth.

She went on: 'How did you hear about the church? Did someone invite you?'

I was defeated. I had to answer now or it would be rude. 'Winston invited me.' I looked at her face to catch her reaction—every stranger always had a reaction—but there wasn't even a flinch. She looked at me as if I were a normal human being as if she hadn't heard an impediment.

'Aww... Winston, yes, he's not here yet, but I'm sure he's on his way. Sit right here, and I'll tell him you are here when he arrives.'

I said, 'Thank you,' and totally relaxed. How friendly was she? Wow. She didn't make me feel as if I were different; I liked it there already.

A few minutes passed, and I caught a glimpse of Winston coming in from a side door. Lisa approached him, and when he looked up, he had the biggest smile. He beckoned to a woman behind him, and they headed towards me. 'Hey, you made it. Aww, man, I didn't think you'd come. I'm so happy to see you. Meet my wife, Sabryna.'

I smiled at them both, and I felt rather overwhelmed.

Sabryna smiled, said hello, and told me to come and sit with them, as they sat more to the middle rather than in the back. I got up, and as we took our places, the service began. The songs were so wonderful, and the music? It was nothing I ever imagined church music to be. Everyone either had their arms raised or were clapping hands. The energy was so good.

The pastor was a visiting pastor, and he had me captivated from the beginning. He spoke on broken vessels and how God is the Master Potter, and we are clay, that he takes us cracked, breaks us, melts us and remoulds us stronger than before. He spoke of the power of love, and how it conquers a multitude of sins.

I sat very quietly.

At the end of the service, some people went to the front to kneel and pray, and there were some who hugged and spoke to them. Nearly all the people who listened had tears, and the ones who spoke smiled. It was a strange sight.

Sabryna asked if I wanted to go up to the front, but I declined. The less I was seen and heard, the better.

Winston seemed a little disappointed that I didn't go up to the front, but he smiled, still thankful that I had come.

They dropped me home and said they could pick me up the next night for the second day. It was a revival, which meant there would be a different service every day for four days. I didn't realise I'd spoken so much to Sabryna; she was absolutely lovely, and I thought she was the perfect wife for Winston.

As promised, they came to collect me the next day. I left the children at home with Ken. It was a school night, and I wanted some time out on my own.

Just like the day before, the church was busy, and the worship music was so good. The worship team, the music—everything was amazing. The pastor preached on the effects of unforgiveness and bitterness and how it is related to certain illnesses and diseases. He spoke of the healing power of the love of Jesus and how God loved us so much that He gave His son to die for us. I knew about God, Jesus and the Trinity, which was standard knowledge, but the way he broke it down was different, and it made total sense. He spoke of God's promises to us and quoted a scripture that has stuck with me. It was Jeremiah 29:11-13 that stated,

> For I know the plans I think toward you, says the Lord, thoughts of peace and not of evil, to give you a future and a hope. Then you will call upon Me and go and pray to Me, and I will listen to you. And you will seek Me and find Me, when you search for Me with all your heart.

I felt consumed. I wanted healing so badly that when the pastor asked who wanted Jesus in their hearts and to be healed from the past, I raised my hand whilst every head was bowed. The pastor looked at me and asked if I meant it. I nodded, and he encouraged me to get out of my chair and go down to the front.

A lady stood with me. She told me to repeat the words she spoke, and I did. I knew, in my heart, that

Jesus understood my speech. I felt He knew my voice, regardless of any impediment, and an overwhelming feeling came over me. My eyes filled with tears, and the lady beside me smiled, and the lady beside me smiled and I remembered this part of the service from the day before!

The lady put her arms around me, introduced herself as Michelle, and told me that everything was going to be okay. They sang a lovely song about the cleansing blood of Jesus as the service came to an end. Wow. What just happened?

A young Asian girl came up to me after service with the biggest smile. Actually, it was more of a grin. She seemed so excited. 'Congratulations! You got saved. That's awesome.'

I was confused. What had she meant?

'You went to the altar and gave your life to Jesus.'

'Oh, yes. Thank you.' I searched to see where Win and Sabryna were standing as I felt safe and not as intimidated when I was near them, but the girl was persistent and continued to tell me how much my life would change and that I would receive a miracle healing and how God loved me so much. She was a lovely girl but overly chatty and bubbly. Definitely filled with the joy of the Lord.

The other girl that had come to the altar to speak to me and lead me in prayer had a gentle, kind nature about her, and she spoke to me for a while. She was so patient as she waited for me to get my words out. In fact, they were all so nice. I felt so accepted with my disability to the point where I forgot that anything was wrong with me.

The third night, Win and Sabryna came to collect me again. This time, I brought the children with me. They had two young boys roughly the same ages as my three and a seven-seater car. Ethan was small, so we were able to squeeze in the extra child.

When we got to the church, quite a few familiar faces came to say hello to me and the children, which made them feel very welcome. They had a children's church that ran at the same time as the main service, so I sent my lot along with the rest of them.

Once again, the service was amazing. The pastor went further into the powers of healing and that we, as children of God, had the power to heal. Many other people were 'saved' that night, and I understood the tears and smiles now.

After the service, Win introduced me to a few more people. He was particularly excited for me to meet an elder in another branch of their church. When the person turned around, every part of me shuddered. I wanted to run. I wanted to hide. I wanted to be sick. What kind of church was this? Was this a joke?

Ethan was standing at my feet when I literally froze. Win said, 'Don't you remember Edmond?' with a smile beaming across his face.

'Edmond, look who it is. Can you believe it? We're all here, saved—how many years later? Who would've thought?'

Edmond shone a smile. 'Oh, my goodness. Is that Maria? Wow, hi, sis. It's been a long time. It's so good to see you.'

Was the guy seriously going to act as if nothing had happened? He looked straight through me as if he had no idea what I might be upset about. Although I did not show it, to be honest, I was so taken aback by his calm, casual outward look that I was silenced.

Winston started to explain to Edmond about the stroke and the symptoms it had left me with. Edmond turned to say that he would pray for my healing right there and then.

What was I hearing? I was not about to let him lay any kind of hands on me. That was the guy who had touched me indecently in the worst way as a young teenager. The one that, after the ordeal, caused me to get licks from my mum as my niece had told her there was a boy in the house, the one whose touch made me feel dirty and soiled and started my need for scalding hot baths.

Had I heard right? Winston had said he was an elder of the church. What the heck was that? I assumed it meant something important like being the pastor's right-hand man or something. Anyway, how was it even possible that the church could be run by womanisers who had no regard for who they damaged?

I was apprehensive, but Edmond reassured me that God was going to make me talk again, and Ethan looked up, excited that he might see some kind of God magic or something.

I decided to go with the flow. I wasn't the type of person to rant and rave in public, and it seemed Edmond was oblivious to anything he'd done to me. Was that God? Could He take such a dark horse like Edmond and change him so completely? I'd found hope three days ago, and it was being swept away from me as quickly as it had come.

Edmond asked about the chain and pendant I wore around my neck. A gift from my brother-in-law, the pendant depicted the patron saint of nervous diseases; my brother-in-law was a Catholic.

'Nope,' Edmond said, 'take that off and throw it away. Healing comes from God, not the images we wear.' There were a good few people around us, including the pastor who had preached. All who were near enough laid their hands on me, and the rest stretched their hands out towards me and started praying. Edmond prayed mostly in English, but most of the others prayed in different languages. I couldn't make out where they'd come from, whether parts of Africa or elsewhere.

I closed my eyes, tried to clear my head and just asked God to work for me.

The praying stopped, and Edmond said, 'Say something.'

Well, what?

Ethan tugged on my skirt and said, 'Say "hospital." You can't say "hospital."' which was true. I pronounced it something like 'harspidial'. So, I opened my mouth and said, 'Horspidal… horspi… hosspidal… hospital… HOSPITAL!'

OMG—was that real?

Ethan was jumping up and down. 'Say "Nadia," say "Nadia."'

'Narrrrdyah... Narrrdayah... Nadyarrr... Nadeeear... Nadia! Nadia! Nadia!' I jumped up and down, laughing and crying at once. I hadn't been able to say my daughter's name in five months.

Everyone cheered and clapped. Pastor Dilly said, 'Say "Jesus."'

'Jayzus... Jeeeayzus... Jeeezus... Jeeesus, Jesus... Jesus.'

The whole group was in uproar. Ethan jumped up and down and Pastor Dilly, Edmond, Winston, Sabryna and Michelle all started to pray. There were others, but I was in a daze. I tried to talk again but fell back into the impediment. I was exhausted and felt like I was going to pass out.

The pastor said I'd made huge progress and not to be discouraged that I was not completely healed, but God had shown His healing powers, and sometimes, it was a process. I'd had a taste of who God was and what He could do for me. He encouraged me to keep coming to church and keep praying and believing. What a night.

The excitement in the car going home was electric. Winston couldn't stop going on about it. He talked and laughed about how great God was for the whole car ride home. Me? All I could think of was how a teenager who had made me feel so dirty and was one of the reasons why my sex life was so screwed up had become a decent

Christian man who respected others, especially women, and who prayed for people's healing. It was mind-boggling. How was that possible?

On the last night of the revival meeting, Pastor Dilly preached a message on the gift of speaking in tongues and how the Holy Spirit interceded for us when we couldn't find the words to pray or needed specific details. When we prayed in tongues, it was a heavenly language that spoke directly to God exactly what needed to be said, for our spirits know more about what we need or desire… or something like that. He explained about the first day of Pentecost and the experience in the Upper room, and I realised that what I'd been hearing in church was not voices of different nationalities but them speaking and praying in tongues.

By the end of the service, I'd also put my hands up to receive that gift. After a while, I started to say things I didn't understand. It just flowed out of me like a cup overflowing. My goodness, what a week.

Over the weeks that followed, Sabryna and Michelle came over, and we chatted and shared things. They were a tower of strength. Ken was sometimes around, but he kept himself away from us. I started attending the church more often. It was so vibrant: the music, the preaching, the people. It was where life was.

Going to that church made the weeks leading up to my break to Trinidad easier.

Ken agreed to drive me to Heathrow Airport. I got big hugs and kisses from the children when they left to go to school. I was going for three weeks, but I promised to call them often.

It was time for me to leave, but Ken wouldn't get up. He just sat there in the living room. Getting upset caused my speech to mess up, so I tried hard to stay calm. He just sat there, looked at me blankly and told me to take myself! Was he really serious? It was past the time I was meant to leave home, and I was panicking.

'Ken, you can't do this. You promised. Sammy is on her way, and I carrrrn't miss myyyyyy flit.' Great. My speech was slipping again. I started to cry and tried speaking again through the tears, but it was pointless.

Ken stood up and got in my face. 'Duh duh duh duh dadadadauhuhuhhu gugugu duhduhduh—'

'SHUT UP!' I began to cry out of frustration and disbelief that he could stoop so low as to ridicule my speech. It was like he was purposely trying to make my speech get worse.

'I'M NOT TAKING YOU. TAKE YOURSELF.' I was in shock. He'd crossed the line. How could he take the mick out of my speech like that? How much more awful could he get?

I rang Sammy, and through tears and broken speech, she eventually caught the drift of things. She doubled back and came to get me. She refused to come in to avoid a fight, so she blew her car horn, and I came out. We were on our way.

The flight was difficult for me at take-off and landing, and I was in tears. It was a mixture of leaving the children, the vertigo and what Ken had done. It was good having Sammy with me. She was livid at Ken's behaviour, but it became more and more apparent that he was going through some sort of breakdown. My mum was going to see to the children whilst I was away, so I felt reassured that they'd be okay.

I called when we arrived, and Ken refused to let me speak to the children, and I just broke down. Sammy took the phone, gave Ken a piece of her mind and made him aware that he wasn't making my road to recovery easier, just delaying it.

The time away was a godsend, and I was able to really meditate, and eat freshly grown food, go to the beach and just relax on a sun lounger. Aunts and cousins looked after us both. I tried to call home a couple of times, but each time, Ken shut me down. Finally, Mum got the children on the phone for me. They were having fun with school friends in the playground and enjoying their grandma's cooking.

Ken called out of the blue in our last week. He said he had five buyers wanting to see the house. Why was he trying to provoke me? How could he put up the house for sale without me? Sammy said he was lying and just being silly. I was tired of this childishness, and I told him to go ahead and let them view it then. It was not what he expected to hear, and he began shouting.

Sammy came over to me. She took the receiver from me and hung up the phone. I saw how accepting Christ was the best decision I'd made, and I hung onto God with all my strength.

I celebrated my thirtieth birthday with Sammy and some cousins. I had a small glass of wine, but because I hadn't touched a drink in months due to my high medication intake, I felt a little giddy straight away. Alcohol was strictly not allowed. I believe it was God slowly taking away my dependency on alcohol so I would depend on him instead. If I hadn't had those TIAs, I think I would've had a major problem with alcohol by then.

I made up my mind that I wasn't going back to fight with Ken anymore. Upon arriving back home, I had a mindset to work at making sure the children were okay and well.

Ken told me the mortgage company had given us four months to sell the house or it would be repossessed. He admitted that his behaviour was unacceptable, and he apologised. Things were not normal, but there was a peaceful truce between us.

There was an evening when Ken must've come to the realisation that we were losing our family home and he wanted to stop the process of selling, but I hadn't want to hear it; it was much too late. He'd given up when I got sick and deliberately stopped working properly or paying the mortgage to spite me, like it was my fault I'd had a stroke. He needed to look long and hard at himself to see the depths of how deep the stress was embedded to have made my body shut down.

We had no way of paying our debts, bills or mortgage. The money we owed to everyone could only come from the sale of the house. 'It's too late, Ken. You stopped paying the mortgage and broke multiple promises of payment. The house is beyond saving now, so get used to the idea that we are about to lose our family home.

'Either they take it, and we are consumed by debt, or we sell and free ourselves from that pressure… and each other! I think we need a time of separation. This is no life for us, and it's unfair for the children to live like this. I want them to be happy. Right now, we all live on eggshells.' I walked away. I was not about to stay and await another argument or fight.

Ken just sat there with his head in his hands. Because of his actions, we were losing our home, and I felt resentful towards him.

After a few disappointments, we finally found a buyer for the house. There was no chain, so it was an easy ride. Due to us going through a legal separation, the profits from the house would be split 60/40 in favour of me as I was keeping the children. Ken went into a fit of rage upon hearing this as he wanted it to be straight down the middle, and, as usual, things were thrown around the room. He picked up one of his speaker boxes to drop on the floor. It was like watching Dr Bruce Banner turn into the Incredible Hulk!

'KEN, STOP!'

He looked at me, still holding the box. I saw the fury in his eyes but at the same time, saw deep sadness. He put down the speaker box, sat down, hung his head and rested it in his hands. A part of my heart softened, and I wanted to reach out, but it was too late. We'd gone too far to turn back.

The papers were signed, and the house was sold. We started to pack and throw away the things we didn't need. The garage was full of baby equipment, a bottle warmer and steamer, a cot and a Moses basket, an old children's wardrobe, old bikes, old toys and more. It was really tiring work, and all the stress was making me tired and ill. Because of my health and my inability to lift heavy things, our close friends, my brothers and Cam helped with the clearing out and packing. Ken was going to stay with his best friend, and I was going to rent privately. I was too scared to buy somewhere else. Plus, I was still out of work - who would give me a mortgage with no income except for sick pay?

Bernel could not believe we still had so many baby things and laughed at our hoarding. 'Wow, was you planning another one?' She laughed, and all I could do was smile. I had, in fact, wanted five children at least and a marriage with longevity, something that would see us celebrating past our twenty-fifth or thirtieth anniversary, but my dreams were dashed.

'Maria, it will be okay. It will be okay. Just thank God you're not pregnant.'

My ears pricked, and a sudden panic arose in me. Ken kept sneaking into the bedroom every so often. I was heavily sedated by bedtime and a lot of quarrels were about him taking advantage of that. The tiredness, the feeling sick. What if I was?

No… my mind was working overtime. God wouldn't play with me like that. It was Friday. I would just wait over the weekend to see if my mind was playing tricks on me.

Friday night. Yep, I felt queasy and very tired, and my appetite had gone. Was it real, though, or was the thought of being pregnant scaring me into a phantom pregnancy?

Saturday. We continued packing. The children were at Mum's. There wasn't a lot more to do. The new owners agreed that I could leave a few of my things in the garage whilst waiting for the money to come through from the sale of the house to pay the deposit and rent of the property I was going to let.

I was quiet for most of the day, anticipating nausea and tiredness to creep up by late afternoon. I decided to forget about it, to just concentrate on clearing the house. Sammy said the kids and I could stay with her until the house we were going to rent came through. Ken refused to help me look for a place to rent. He simply didn't care, not even for the children's sake.

By the evening, all I could do was cry.

When morning came, I went to the pharmacy before going to church and bought a Clear Blue pregnancy test. I got home, and even my pee was scared to come down! Finally—and after the longest three minutes ever—there it was: a very prominent cross.

The children and I got to church. We now attended Winston's church regularly, and the kids loved it, too. I paced up and down in reception, waiting for Sabryna to arrive. We had become really tight friends, and I confided in her a lot.

There she was. I ran up to her and grabbed her arm to pull her to the side. 'Sabryna, something bad has happened. My life is over. I don't understand why God would do this.' I sobbed, like really sobbed. Sabryna was still recovering from my grabbing her so swiftly.

'Slow down, Maria. What's happening—happened—what's wrong? Slow down.'

'I'm pregnant,' and with that, I cried again.

'Oh, sweetheart. Is that it? Don't worry, my darling. I know it is not the right time, but God always has a plan.' Again, that Bible scripture, Jeremiah 29:11, came to mind, soothing me: '"For I know the plans I have for you," declares the Lord, "plans to prosper you and not to harm you, plans to give you hope and a future."'

Sabryna hugged me and told me about God's gift of pregnancy. She knew all about the sale of the house and Ken and I separating. She knew of the turbulence in our home. She knew everything, yet she said that God had a plan!

My crying began to die down. I'd needed it to come out. The tears had been a mixture of everything bottled up within me, and now, I'd had a release. Sabryna promised to be there for me every step of the way, and the sisters in the church and the pastors would be there to support me and the children.

The pregnancy couldn't have come at a worse time, but it was here, and one thing I knew without a shadow of a doubt: I wasn't going to put it to sleep!

Finally, later that week, myself and the children went to stay at Sammy's. It was quite cramped, but it was only for a little while. She was amazing and helped me get the children to school when she was on late shift.

Ken moved in with his best friend on the other side of London and took the kids every other weekend to his sister's to spend time with them. It was strange at first, but I was free of the fighting, tension, frustration, rejection, hatred and debt. I say hatred, but I still loved who we used to be, still loved him to a certain degree. He was my first and only true love, as true as I could get.

Ken was devastated when I told him about the pregnancy. I was six weeks into it at the time. Tears ran down his face. He had lost everything, and this would be the first pregnancy we would not share. He sunk deeper into depression.

It was the summer holidays, and Ken had promised to pick up the kids that Friday to spend a long weekend. As much as we fought, he still tried to be a good dad, and the kids loved him so much. On Tuesday, Ken called me to say he could not come on Fridays any more. He said he'd booked a flight out to the Grenadines and was leaving on Thursday.

'How long for? Just like that? But you promised the children.'

There was a long silence. 'Six months. I need to get out. I can't cope. I can't cope.'

'But what about the baby? You're going to leave me to do this on my own: the children, labour, EVERYTHING?' The panic I felt was mixed with anger. 'You SELFISH BASTARD! I HATE YOU.'

'Look, you'll be okay. You have family. My sister Stella—she is always there for you—and you got them church people who are always sniffing around.'

'Sniffing around? They are doing MORE THAN YOU.' I stopped as I heard my speech begin to waiver, and I had learnt to stop and take control.

'Look, Maria, you're gonna have to tell the kids. I CAN'T DO IT, I'M SORRY.' With that, he hung up the phone, and I stood there, dumbfounded.

Luckily, Stella had encouraged Ken to come to see the children as he would have caused them too much pain if he just vanished. He told them he was going on a long holiday to see Grandma and Granddad and would be back before they knew it. They were all in tears. It was a sorrowful scene, and I cried, too, not for me but the children and the new baby.

Ken left; I was on my own.

Weeks flowed into months. We settled into our new home, and the kids were in a good school. It was a bit of a distance: one bus to the train station, then two stops on the train. The heavier I got in the pregnancy, the more difficult it got travelling until I just couldn't do it anymore. Nadia was now in charge. She was 10 years old and very sensible. They knew the route, and I had to let them travel it on their own, as I was still too sick to be allowed to drive.

Sabryna was right. Literally, nearly all the church helped out, took me shopping for groceries, took me to doctor and hospital appointments, picked us up for church and dropped us back after fellowships. Sabryna happily agreed to be my birthing partner when the time arrived for me to give birth, so no, I wouldn't be on my own. She never stopped encouraging me and was always there, if not in person, then via the phone. She had first joined the church as a single parent. Her boys were not Winston's, so she had them out of wedlock in a previous relationship, so she knew firsthand the stigma I felt being a single mum. The church was Pentecostal, and neither believed nor taught sex before marriage.

I became more independent and grew as a Christian. The more I listened to sermons, the more I was able to reach back into my past and forgive the acts of abuse, rejection and negativity thrown at me. I noticed something miraculous, too: the joint pain ceased. I was free and healed from my fibromyalgia. There is no cure for it in modern medicine, but in Jesus, I was healed. It was related to unforgiveness and bitterness, and my healing came gradually as I gradually buried my past hurts.

I was a new me. I still talked funny, but I was getting easier to understand. I even started to teach myself how to cook again. It wasn't cordon bleu, but it was something, and the children were finally eating MY home-cooked meals. We'd made it. We were overcomers.

It was two months before Ken made contact again. He sounded much better and, dare I say, a lot like how he was in the early days. He had come out of the worst of his depression and was more like his normal self, mentally speaking. We were able to talk civilly, and the children enjoyed his calls. I told him about the baby's growth and how the church and Sabryna were supporting us. This saddened him as he knew they were doing what he rightfully should. I also told him that Sabryna was my birthing partner, so I wouldn't be alone. It would be the first childbirth he wouldn't be there for.

There was a long silence. 'No, I'll be there.' He said it as if he truly meant it.

I was 37 weeks when I went into labour. We were at a gospel concert, and all of a sudden, a pain suddenly kicked in. Sabryna happened to look over at me, grabbed our coats and laughed, saying there was no way my waters were going to bust out there.

Winston dropped us to the hospital and took my children back with him. I cried. Deep down, I wanted Ken, and Sabryna knew it. She was so good in comforting me, and, as promised, she called Ken to tell him I had gone into labour.

After a few hours, I had not dilated, and the midwife said it could be the Braxton Hicks preparing my body for labour. She said I could go home as it was a false alarm!

Win came to collect us and took me home. Sabryna didn't like how I was and as a precaution, decided to stay with me. It was the next day when the contractions began again. That time, they were stronger and in no way could be Braxton Hicks. They were 10 minutes apart.

Sabryna held my hands and allowed me to squeeze them when the pain of the contractions came. Then, just like that, the pain faded.

The midwife checked and said I was four centimetres dilated, so it was happening but slowly. It was another half hour before the pain kicked in again. That time, I needed the Entonox. The gas and air concoction was a godsend and left me in a natural high with each bout of pain.

The door opened, and Sabryna gasped. I saw the silhouette of a man, but I was too spaced out to see clearly. 'Hello, I told you I'd be here.'

'Ken?'

Sabryna let gently go my hand and smiled at me. 'You see? God always has a plan!

'Ken, come—you need to do this. I think she needs you.' She looked at me. 'You okay? I can stay if you want, but I don't want to be in the way. It's okay. We've done this whole journey together. This is the last relay. Let me pass the baton to Ken for the last leg.' She kissed my forehead and told me to call her as soon as possible after the baby was born as she would be waiting.

She went up to Ken. 'Well done.' she said. She smiled and left, and it was just me and him.

It was hard to talk through the pain. He told me not to think about things now, just concentrate on the pain and the labour. Somehow, his being there made me calm. Our baby wouldn't be the odd one out after all. Its daddy was present for the birth.

Three hours later and she was here: six pounds, four ounces and healthy. Asian curly hair and ever so pretty. Ken looked at me, said, 'Sorry,' with tears in his eyes, and kissed me gently on the lips. 'Thank you,' he whispered.

The children were ecstatic when they saw their dad and nearly forgot they had a new sister. If I could compare it to a season, I felt like it would be spring: new buds, new flowers, fresh mornings, early bees humming, birds singing and beautiful butterflies fluttering their wings against the light breeze. How wonderful for the butterfly. When you really stop to think, they spend the first part of their lives as ugly creatures, crawling on their bellies, then they go through a transformation, and at the opportune time, the right time, they break out of their cocoons and fly.

Could that be it? Had we just broken out of our cocoon? It had been an enclosed space of hurt, betrayal, rejection, loneliness, pressure and suffocation. Were we now free?

Only time would tell what was to be. If God had a plan, His promise was that it would not harm us, so in Him, I decided to put my trust.

My wings are out!

OUT FLEW THE BUTTERFLY...

Something changed in me today
Something's unfolded and rearranged
That which was locked within, churning at my bones
Has seeped through the cracks of my invisible ozone
My atmosphere is clear
Even though words in print were like a dagger to the eyes
It became my greatest inspiration, allowing me to inhale, to rise
To inspire is to breathe life into a burnt-out shell and stimulate the spirit as it battled demons from hell
As this great inspiration fills me with the urge and ability to elevate, to strive, my hopes are resurrected
I exhale... I AM alive!
To aspire
Aspiration now directs and has awoken the intellect, ambitious to achieve, to rise to the highest high
I soar...
As powerful as an eagle
I fly out as God opens the door
No longer does negativity affect me
Happiness is my best friend.
Blurred vision causes one to stumble
And fear of making the wrong move causes failure...
Clear vision gives power, and as I step forward, I regain authority and control
I am a survivor...
I step like a warrior
I advance like a soldier

I have the power to inspire
And the ability to aspire
I replace neglect and reject with love and protect
Arrows pass me by
I fought on one spot with my eyes wide shut
All I did was shout the name JESUS, and the fighting stopped!...
Fear has dissolved, it had lost its salt and has no effect
My antenna no longer detects the weapons of warfare that sang the same battle cry over and over and over and over again
No longer am I subject to the things you do—
I am the one who has power over you
God came, and He conquered and showed me how to overcome
For years an ugly caterpillar, I eventually crawled into a cocoon, and there, metamorphosis began
Then, when I least expected, when I thought all hope was gone
Out flew the butterfly; how beautiful am I?

YES, I have the victory
God's plan was that I should overcome
My wings of salvation have developed
Dookie Dooks, you've won
Now, go live your life
Redeemed and restored by God's Son

Yours sincerely,
Loving you always,

Me xx

ABOUT THE AUTHOR

Alison Ryan-Chase is the author of the poetry collection *Downloads From Heaven* and the memoir *Out Flew the Butterfly*, her second book. A mother of five, affectionately known as "Granny Ali" to her grandchildren, Alison is also a proud mother-in-law of two.

Married and divorced twice, Alison's life has been marked by both trials and triumphs. After suffering a stroke in 1999 that left her without speech, cognitive function, or motor skills, she defied the odds by teaching herself to talk, walk, and return to her greatest passion: cooking.

Despite enduring ill health, the pain of marital breakdowns, and the devastating loss of her beloved brother in 2012, Alison went on to achieve a Bachelor of Science degree in Environmental Health—one of her proudest accomplishments.

A professional chef with over 35 years of experience, Alison is now the personal chef behind the fine dining business Fooderella, where she continues to share her love of food and resilience with every dish.

Conscious Dreams
PUBLISHING

Transforming diverse writers
into successful published authors

✉ www.consciousdreamspublishing.com

✉ authors@consciousdreamspublishing.com

Let's connect

www.ingramcontent.com/pod-product-compliance
Lightning Source LLC
Chambersburg PA
CBHW030306080526
44584CB00012B/457